# WORKING
## with the
# LABYRINTH

# WORKING
## *with the*
# LABYRINTH

## Paths for exploration

Ruth Sewell, Jan Sellers and Di Williams

**wild goose**
publications

www.**ionabooks**.com

First published 2012
Wild Goose Publications, 4th Floor, Savoy House, 140 Sauchiehall St,
Glasgow G2 3DH, UK.
Wild Goose Publications is the publishing division of the Iona Community.
Scottish Charity No. SC003794. Limited Company Reg. No. SC096243.
www.ionabooks.com

ISBN 978-1-84952-246-5

The publishers gratefully acknowledge the support of the Drummond Trust,
3 Pitt Terrace, Stirling FK8 2EY in producing this book.

Overseas distribution:
*Australia:* Willow Connection Pty Ltd, Unit 4A, 3-9 Kenneth Road,
Manly Vale, NSW 2093
*New Zealand:* Pleroma, Higginson Street, Otane 4170, Central Hawkes Bay
*Canada:* Bayard Distribution, 49 Front Street East, Toronto, Ontario M5E 1B3

Printed by Bell & Bain, Thornliebank, Glasgow

# Contents

# Foreword

KIMBERLY LOWELLE SAWARD

The labyrinth is an ancient symbol that is enjoying renewed popularity in modern times. I first encountered it in 1995 when I visited Grace Cathedral, a beautiful San Francisco landmark where a large walkable labyrinth fills the floor of the nave. Seeing the labyrinth for the first time, splashed in dappled colour as sunlight poured through the cathedral's stained-glass windows, set fire to my soul. I experienced a delightful sense of recognition and familiarity.

The labyrinth symbol has a long but vague history that encircles the globe and weaves with subtle grace through the ages of humankind. Archaeological evidence illustrates the grasp the labyrinth has held on our collective imagination for more than four thousand years. An archetype in the sense that it transcends the boundaries of both time and culture, the labyrinth appears in diverse locations around the world, accompanied by stories and practices that feed the heart and spirit. I have been fortunate enough to travel throughout the world in search of the labyrinth symbol wherever it can be found, in settings both modern and ancient. That travel has shown me again and again that something profound happens when an individual meets a labyrinth and experiences its effect on a deep and wordless level. Again and again, history has shown that, once encountered, the labyrinth is inevitably taken onwards to new communities where it is adapted to fit local customs and materials, and is adopted into the heart of its new home.

Labyrinths create community just as much as they are created by communities, bringing together people from various walks in life, bridging traditional barriers such as age, geography, religion, profession and income. This book is, itself, a reflection of the labyrinth's community-building nature ... the authors of the various chapters have met and become friends through their association with the labyrinth, the result being this volume you now hold in your hands, a tangible example of diverse interests weaving together to illustrate a multifaceted concept.

I love walking the meandering pathways that lead toward the

centre, where I know I will also find my own centre, and where I will pause before beginning my outward walk, eventually stepping out of the labyrinth and back into my daily life. For me, the labyrinth is a safe container for imaginal experience; I go to the labyrinth to experience my own interiority. That is my way ...

My way is but one of many, however. There are as many reasons for visiting labyrinths as there are people who seek them out. Among others, artists, historians, peace workers and health-care professionals find that labyrinths feed their work, while spiritual seekers and those in need of strength or support find it feeds their souls. For many of us, the labyrinth can hold whatever we bring to it, be it a heart seeking solace, an impassioned prayer, a creative spirit looking for inspiration, a body in need of a place to play, or simply a curious mind.

Wherever we may be in our own life journeys, the labyrinth has something to teach us. Bringing imagination to the path we are treading invokes soul into the journey. Our personal journey then gives shape to our culture and the global community to which we all belong.

*Kimberly Lowelle Saward, PhD*

## About the author

Kimberly Lowelle Saward, Ph.D., taught psychology at Sonoma State University in California and worked clinically as a school counsellor and somatic therapist. Bringing her perspective as a lifelong student of spiritual practice, pilgrimage and sacred sites, she has been working with labyrinths since 1995. She is currently researching modern and historic uses of the labyrinth, exploring its role in folk customs, mythology and spiritual development.

Kimberly is the author of *Ariadne's Thread: Legends of the Labyrinth*, a psycho-spiritual study of labyrinth practices worldwide. Co-founder and director of Labyrinthos, she travels widely and served as president of the international Labyrinth Society.

Introduction

In our busy world, there is a pressing need for quietness, for breathing space. We all fulfil different roles, often many different roles each day, and find ourselves racing to meet – or attempt to meet – our commitments. This book is based on the principle that we all, whoever we are, need time for quietness and reflection, time for stillness, time to refresh our energies and our spirits.

There is an ancient artefact, the labyrinth, which can help to meet such a need. Around the world, a growing number of people are working with it. This book is designed for labyrinth enthusiasts in many different contexts – especially those who are introducing the labyrinth to others. It will also be of interest to anyone who would like to explore different approaches and find out more about the possibilities of this remarkable resource.

## What is a labyrinth?

A labyrinth is an ancient pattern like a complex spiral, usually (unlike a maze) with just one path to the centre and out again. These patterns have been found across the world, in many countries and cultures. The oldest found so far, carved on a rock face in Spain, dates back some four thousand years (1). Labyrinths appear in different forms, from Roman mosaic to pottery and from ancient coins to turf or stone labyrinths with the pattern laid out on the ground. Since the 1970s, an international resurgence of interest has led to the construction of many labyrinths in public or private spaces and to the use of portable or transient materials, from canvas labyrinths to leaves and sand. Accessible as a permanent or temporary installation, the labyrinth provides a meditative walk that nurtures the spirit, deepening reflection and creativity and sometimes leading to unexpected insights.

This book offers ideas and examples of labyrinths in use in arts, community and social settings; schools, colleges and universities; a hospice, and a secure hospital; counselling, psychotherapy and well-being; churches, retreats and interfaith contexts. We hope that readers will glean ideas for their own field of activity, experiment with ideas from other fields and go on to share their own enjoyment and enthusiasm, as we have aimed to do in this book.

## Why this book; why now?

The editors – Ruth Sewell, Jan Sellers and Di Williams – first met in Chartres, France in 2008. Di was co-teaching the Veriditas Facilitator Training programme with the Revd Dr Lauren Artress; Jan and Ruth were there to train as labyrinth facilitators. All three left Chartres with a passion to develop labyrinth work in the UK.

Through their networking, they became aware of the need for a text that would focus on the practical experience of those already working with labyrinths in various contexts. They understand the sharing of such experience is invaluable for trainee and certified facilitators and for those involved in new labyrinth projects, as well as being of interest to labyrinth enthusiasts everywhere. This, then, is a book for the enrichment of those working with labyrinths – a book to nurture imagination and to deepen knowledge of resources and possibilities.

The editors are aware of the importance of good in-depth training for people wishing to offer the labyrinth for others. Currently, the most comprehensive training in the UK is offered by Veriditas (2). Through this non-profit organisation, committed to introducing people to the wisdom of the labyrinth, there is now a growing community of trained and certified facilitators advancing understanding and practice.

There are many talented labyrinth-makers, teachers and facilitators in the UK and worldwide. The editors' task was to seek out chapters from authors that would reflect the depth of seasoned experience in the UK. Given the wide range of uses of the labyrinth, it was a challenge for us to decide what should go into this volume; we therefore chose those authors and subjects we thought would reflect current themes and areas of development in the UK. It was also our intention that this book would serve as a resource for those training to be labyrinth stewards, builders or facilitators. In addition, we were influenced by our knowledge of those organisations and institutions in the UK that are welcoming the construction of permanent labyrinths or using temporary labyrinths within their services, examples of which are explored in the following chapters.

## In this book ...

Our Foreword is written by *Dr Kimberly Lowelle Saward*, a founding member of the Labyrinth Society (3). Kimberly's scholarly experience and writing reflect her knowledge of the labyrinth across many continents. Kimberly reminds us of the antiquity of this archetypal pattern, and the depth and beauty of the experiences to be found through a labyrinth walk. No matter where the labyrinth is found, it brings people together across boundaries and is readily adapted to new communities and different cultures.

## Chapter 1: Constructing Temporary and Permanent Labyrinths
*Jeff Saward*

Jeff is one of the world's leading authorities on the history and development of labyrinths and mazes. Those familiar with Jeff's work will be aware of his commitment to scholarly research and to public understanding of this field, as exemplified in his wide-ranging publications. This chapter offers a practical, detailed and expert guide to the construction of temporary and permanent labyrinths from many different resources – a feast for the imagination.

## Chapter 2: Children, Young People and Labyrinths
*Rosemary Norton*

Rosemary is a teacher and a psychotherapist who works in schools with children aged five to eighteen. Her chapter illustrates how to engage children in the creation of a labyrinth, indoors or outdoors, with simple materials to aid the process. For some children this is a spiritual experience, and many find a relaxed and reflective inner space. Rosemary's insightful work supports both the learning environment and the learning process.

## Chapter 3: Universities and Colleges
*Jan Sellers*

Jan's pioneering work with labyrinths in higher education has been recognised in the UK and beyond, and led to the construction of the Canterbury Labyrinth, at the University of Kent's Canterbury campus. Jan continues to support others to bring such opportunities to students and staff alike, exploring labyrinths within the curriculum, creativity, student transition and wellbeing, staff development and more, as illustrated in this chapter.

## Chapter 4: In Search of the Unattended Shadow
*Jim Buchanan*

Jim trained as a landscape architect and his work is recognised worldwide. Jim explores the boundaries of form and material, and the artistic and creative dynamic of installing a labyrinth. The labyrinth has great potency as a source of inspired artwork; this is evocatively described in Jim's chapter, which includes a sequence of developmental drawing exercises for the reader, leading us step by step from small-scale drawing to community initiatives.

## Chapter 5: Labyrinths in Hospices
*Lizzie Hopthrow*

Lizzie's dedicated work was central to the integration of the labyrinth into the spiritual and pastoral services for patients, relatives and visitors attending the Pilgrims Hospice in Canterbury, Kent. She shares here a personal account of this journey, from the use of finger labyrinths to the construction of a permanent outdoor labyrinth. Lizzie reflects on the results of this initiative, illustrated by the major contribution the labyrinth makes to the work of the hospice.

Chapter 6: Churches, Retreats and Spirituality Centres
*Di Williams*

Di has inspired many through her work as a trainer of labyrinth facilitators. In 2010 she became the first Veriditas-trained Master Teacher in the UK. As University Chaplain, Di initiated and drove forward the creation of the Edinburgh Labyrinth, the permanent outdoor labyrinth at the University of Edinburgh. In this chapter Di draws on her extensive experience of 'spiritual paths', the use of the labyrinth in different spiritual settings.

Chapter 7: Community and Public Labyrinths
*David Kelf*

The revival of interest in labyrinths is reflected in the construction of public labyrinths. One fine example is that of the labyrinth in Seaton, Devon, built to celebrate the town's millennium. David, along with local colleagues, advocated and successfully guided the construction of the labyrinth, beautifully situated in a park overlooking Lyme Bay. For those who want to support or develop a local initiative, this detailed account gives advice that will prove invaluable.

Chapter 8: The Freedom of a Labyrinth in a Secure Setting
*Catherine Moon*

This chapter explores the use of labyrinths in a mental health context. Catherine was ordained at Grace Cathedral, San Francisco, where she first encountered labyrinths. She is now an Anglican chaplain at Ashworth Hospital, Liverpool, where she has introduced the labyrinth as a healing and liberating space in this high-security environment. Her vision and determination led to the creation of a garden labyrinth at Ashworth, the first of its kind in the UK.

**Chapter 9: The Labyrinth in Stress Management and Self-Care**
*Ruth Sewell*

Ruth is a psychotherapist who has also specialised in holistic approaches to health and well-being. This chapter grew out of one of her personal development workshops, 'Gentle Space'. The chapter explores ways and means for personal exploration: ways to access and maintain connection to inner space and inner stillness. Through incorporating a labyrinth walk into such workshops, Ruth has witnessed many people find this connection to what nurtures them.

## Working with the labyrinth: paths for exploration

We hope you will find *Working with the Labyrinth* a book to browse and return to, a source of ideas and inspiration. Like a labyrinth, it will take unexpected twists and turns: we'd like to encourage readers to explore settings and contexts very different from their own, where labyrinth initiatives may offer surprising connections and possibilities.

We are delighted to have gathered contributions from such diverse enthusiasts, and hope that this book will serve as a helpful resource for anyone who – new to labyrinths, or expert – is looking for fresh ideas and ways forward in introducing, creating and working with labyrinths.

## References

1. Saward, Jeff (2003). *Labyrinths and Mazes: The definitive guide to ancient and modern traditions*. London: Gaia.
2. Veriditas website: *www.veriditas.org*
3. The Labyrinth Society website: *www.labyrinthsociety.org/*

# Constructing Temporary and Permanent Labyrinths

JEFF SAWARD

Labyrinths hold an appeal for all, for the seeker looking to address serious purpose with symbolic creativity, as well as playful souls who build for the sheer delight of making and walking. Designing and building your own labyrinth, be it a temporary or permanent installation, is not as difficult as might at first appear. With a little imagination and good preparation, combined with determination and available materials, there is no limit to what can be achieved. This chapter will furnish ideas to help you to find your own ways of constructing temporary or more permanent labyrinths.

## Temporary structures

Creating a labyrinth on a beach, scratched into wet sand with a stick, is without doubt one of the easiest – albeit temporary – methods, and will always amuse the children, as well as the child within. The classical labyrinth symbol (starting with a cross, four angles and four dots) is the ideal starting point and, once committed to memory, will allow you to develop your labyrinth creation skills and play with the alternative forms that can be created. While a tape measure might be required for larger, more complex designs, a standard unit of path width, fashioned from a stick or piece of flotsam, will help ensure consistency of form.

On rockier shorelines, or upland terrains, the building of labyrinths from rocks, boulders and wave-rounded stones from the beach has a long tradition. Historic labyrinths of this type can be found throughout northern Europe, where more than six hundred such labyrinths are recorded (and many still survive), some of which are in excess of five hundred years old. Similar labyrinths, built from whatever rocks were to hand, are known from as far afield as India and Arizona (1). Not surprisingly these stone labyrinths, as easy to build now with little more than a pile of rocks as they have been throughout their long history, are proving a popular choice for the modern labyrinth creator. Equally appealing for gardeners is their low maintenance requirements,

*The construction of a classical labyrinth from the so-called 'seed pattern'. This process has been used for drawing this form of labyrinth throughout history and around the world: Image by Jeff Saward.*

providing the stones are firmly bedded at the outset of the project. Again, a simple temporary labyrinth design can be formed by eye or with a standard measure; the laying out of more intricate forms will benefit from the use of a tape measure.

One of the foremost determinations to be made about a temporary labyrinth is the degree of permanence it will have. A labyrinth of sand may last until the next tide, one formed of stones until it becomes overgrown (or maybe for centuries in certain locations!). Seasonal labyrinths mown into the lawns of large gardens and meadows are popular where long days and pleasant summer evenings invite people to walk the turning paths until fall leaves and winter weather obliterate the patterns. In snowy climes, adventurous creators have been known to create labyrinths on snow-covered ground and frozen lakes – ice skaters can even sharpen their techniques as they glide around the turns – and such frozen labyrinths are ideal sites for candlelit walks and winter celebrations.

For those wanting an even more temporary installation, for a child's party or a one-day or evening event, e.g weddings and other special events, simple labyrinths can be laid out quickly using convenient or themed materials to define the walls. Survey flags, plastic cutlery or feathers can be stuck into the ground; larger items like pinecones or sticks can simply be laid out. With a little forward planning, chopped corn or bird seed can also be poured in lines to mark the walls, and will survive until the local wildlife arrives to feast. A striking centrepiece for an evening garden party or facilitated walk is a labyrinth whose paths are outlined with glowing luminary bags or with lanterns. These can be easily made by placing tea light candles in glass jars or on a bed of sand in small paper sacks (choose fire-resistant versions).

## Permanent installation

Many people are now building more permanent labyrinths in their gardens, or in the grounds of public parks, churches and retreat centres, etc. Constructed with materials ranging from whatever is simple and easily to hand to elegant imported stone requiring professional installation, such labyrinths often reflect the personal and spiritual philosophies of the person or organisation for whom they are built. Local stone, relics with personal significance to stand in the centre, or carefully chosen flowers and herbs can all play an integral role in the project, as can the shape of the winding paths themselves. While classical labyrinths are quick and easy to construct, medieval styles often require more planning and skill to execute. Designs of more contemporary, artistic or figurative forms are also suitable, especially when constructed from natural materials. The regular geometric nature of many labyrinth designs makes them ideal for setting into a tiled floor or close-fitting block pavement. Often smaller in scale than the historic examples found on the floors of churches and cathedrals, the inspiration for so many modern labyrinths, they offer considerable opportunity for personalisation to reflect some combination of the builder, the owner or the setting. A simple square or rectangular labyrinth formed from paving blocks or tiles of contrasting colours is within the scope of any keen amateur builder – a large sheet of graph paper is ideal for designing the pattern and will considerably help with construction. Octagonal designs are visually pleasing, but will require a considerable number of angled cuts. A circular labyrinth set into a pavement invariably calls for the careful selection of materials, will involve more complex cuts, and will probably require the services of a professional installer.

A labyrinth with a pathway formed from small paving slabs (12 inch/30 cm units are ideal), set in concrete for stability, with gravel between the paths is relatively simple to construct. A square design is straightforward enough, and circular labyrinths can also be constructed with the additional use of the sectioned circles and wedges that can be purchased for forming circular pavements. Finding the ideal combination of shapes to form turns and curves will require some experimentation before fixing the slabs in place, but the satisfaction of working out a solution from apparently awkward materials brings its own pleasure, much like solving a puzzle. Forming your labyrinth with smaller blocks or cobbles bounding a gravel path is even simpler, but the need to rake and replenish the gravel will add to the upkeep requirement.

The appreciation of labyrinths in educational settings has become an important feature of the current revival of labyrinth enthusiasm. The creation of labyrinths on school playgrounds and fields, and in public playgrounds, has introduced a new generation of children to the labyrinth symbol and its widespread occurrence and forms. Often, when this is coupled with specific classes or projects, the pupils get to put their new-found knowledge and construction skills to the test. The resulting labyrinth is seen very much as 'their labyrinth', not just an installation provided for their enlightenment or entertainment. It also provides an important springboard for other projects, mathematical, historical and especially arts-based. Creating a labyrinth on a paved or tarmac playground doesn't require expensive equipment or materials. Playground chalks or line-marking paint can fashion a pleasing labyrinth, or simple maze, in little more than a few hours; spray-can aerosol paints can cut the construction time to minutes!

## Practical considerations

Whatever your chosen materials, the width of the paths and the overall size of the labyrinth should be carefully considered at the planning stage. A labyrinth with narrow paths can prove difficult to walk, and while anything much less than 12 inches/30 cm is often considered too narrow, it can also be argued that too wide a path is a distraction from the focus required when walking a labyrinth. In locations where disabled or wheelchair access is important, obviously a wider path will be required, and this may dictate the construction of a labyrinth with fewer circuits to fit the available space. A small labyrinth with three or five circuits can be fitted into a confined space, but a full eleven-circuit replica of a cathedral labyrinth with generous path width will clearly require more room. In such a case the question must be asked ... can a labyrinth be too large? Consider how long you think you might wish to spend walking your labyrinth, and whether potential visitors might have mobility problems. In general, labyrinths much larger than 100 feet/30 metres in diameter are not common.

The orientation of a labyrinth is an important issue for some. Those constructing a replica of the Chartres Cathedral labyrinth might consider it essential to align the principal axis of the labyrinth east/west, in line with the common orientation of Christian churches and cathedrals, but this would be ignoring the fact that the entrance of the labyrinth at Chartres actually faces southwest. Other groups of historical labyrinths sometimes face particular directions, perhaps as a consequence of their typical locations or cultural contexts, but there is no hard and fast rule as to which way a labyrinth should be aligned.

The modern builder might find that in an open location the direction should be influenced by the setting, taking into account the view when standing at either the entrance or centre of the labyrinth, or aligning it on a prominent landmark, stone or tree, or the direction of sunrise or sunset on a significant date. In a garden setting, nearby structures or trees, access to the labyrinth or the direction of first approach might be more important factors. Either way, rather than take a dogmatic approach, it's often best to consider the surroundings and how the labyrinth will be used before making such decisions.

Likewise, the exact position of your labyrinth in the landscape may be important. Dowsing and other geomantic location methods might be employed to select the spot, or you may choose your location simply because it just looks and feels right. Whatever your personal taste or tradition, it is always worth paying close attention to the location and the potential experience of the eventual owner or walkers of your labyrinth.

## Ideas for the garden

The sculptural qualities of deeply cut traditional turf labyrinths have inspired a number of labyrinth builders in recent decades; mounding soil and turf in your own garden to create a labyrinthine path bounded by undulating walls or surrounding a central mound is a viable option for anyone with a strong back, a good shovel, and the willingness to invest some time in the upkeep of the labyrinth. The care and maintenance of a permanent labyrinth in a garden or other open space is always going to be a consideration. Even a simple labyrinth, with paths bounded by trenches dug into the ground, requires regular scouring to keep the invading grass and weeds at bay, although filling the trenches with gravel or bark chips will ease this maintenance issue. A number of designers have constructed turf labyrinths in open grassy areas by setting bricks and paving blocks directly into the turf. A single line of bricks or stone can be simply installed to define the walls of the labyrinth, leaving a wide grass path suitable for summer and dry weather use. A wider line of blocks forming the pathway, with turf ridges in between, will need a firm foundation, but can be walked in all weathers. If it is recessed slightly below the ground surface, it will then be possible to run a lawnmower directly over the blocks without incurring damage. Either way, maintenance is reduced to little more than an occasional clipping back where the turf begins to encroach.

Of course, it is always possible to create a simple labyrinthine pathway leading through raised beds of flowers, providing a colourful diversion in the garden and an excuse to dally on the path to admire the plantings. A labyrinth of herbs, especially flowering varieties, is an old design concept first proposed by garden writers as far back as the sixteenth century. Often invested with much symbolic significance, such labyrinths were certainly built, though unfortunately none survive from this period. In recent times several modern interpretations of this concept have been built in the form of both mazes and labyrinths. To wander between the banks of fragrant herbs, dotted with flowers and alive with insects, is a delight for the senses. Similar projects can be attempted with annual bedding plants and flowers – indeed a simple labyrinth planted with spring flowering bulbs in a lawn area is an ideal way to entice you out into the garden to celebrate the approach of warmer days ahead. Crocuses are ideal and soon die back to leave the lawn open for the summer; a labyrinth formed of daffodils will require more space.

Simpler still is the idea of mowing the pathway of a labyrinth into an open area of longer grass, although this often requires a sizeable lawn or meadow to be effective. A twisting pathway leading through a wildflower meadow allows the visitor to walk between the banks of tall grass and admire the flowers without trampling them. Cutting the grass for the first time early in the season, to establish the pattern, requires some spatial planning and layout skills; a central stake and measured circuits defined by a line of spray paint, sand or chalk dust to guide the lawnmower may prove helpful! However, it is easy to keep the path maintained throughout the summer season by simply mowing the path, ideally the same width as the cut of your lawnmower.

If children are around, however, a more robust approach may be required. One solution that will last for a summer season is to mark the walls of a labyrinth on a lawn with a suitable fertiliser. The first decent rain shower will soon be followed by lush new growth as the fertilised grass shoots longer and darker to this plan for the rest of the season, no matter how frequently the grass is cut. Of course, the use of a traditional solution, such as lime-based tennis court or sports ground paint, is always a possibility, but this can be awkward and messy to apply. Surveyors' spray paint, while usually used for marking out a labyrinth, can also be employed to produce a quick and easy layout that will last until the first heavy rainstorm, or the lawnmower, comes along.

## Conclusion

If you, too, wish to add a labyrinth to your life, be it at your church or your school, in your garden or backyard, or at some lonely spot in the landscape where you walk regularly or which you just happen across while on an excursion or holiday, the simplest solutions are often the best. While employing the services of a design genius, a land artist or a professional installer is sometimes appropriate and necessary, there are always opportunities to do it yourself. Labyrinths can be formed from an infinite variety of materials and installed for temporary one-off use or as permanent features.

The adaptability that has taken labyrinths around the world over thousands of years is as vibrant now as it has always been. The only limits are the bounds of your imagination.

## References

1.  Saward, J. (2002) *Magical Paths – Labyrinths & Mazes in the 21ˢᵗ Century*. London, Mitchell Beazley.

## Recommended Reading and Resources

Buchanan, J. (2007) *Labyrinths for the Spirit*. London, Gaia.
Raphael-Sands, H. (2000) *Labyrinth: Pathway to Meditation and Healing*. London, Gaia.
Saward, J. (2003) *Labyrinths & Mazes*. London, Gaia.

## Websites

Labyrinthos: *www.labyrinthos.net*
The Labyrinth Society: *www.labyrinthsociety.org*
Worldwide Labyrinth Locator: *www.labyrinthlocator.org*

## About the author

First captivated by the labyrinth in 1976, Jeff Saward is a world authority on the history and development of labyrinths and mazes. He is the author of *Magical Paths*, a pictorial essay on the modern revival, and of *Labyrinths & Mazes*, a comprehensive illustrated history, and is the editor of *Caerdroia – the Journal of Mazes and Labyrinths* and co-founder and director of Labyrinthos, the Labyrinth Resource Centre, Photo Library and Archive. Travelling extensively to research the history of labyrinths and mazes, Jeff has an unrivalled collection of photographs of these from around the world and is frequently consulted to provide designs, information, illustrations and documentation for both modern construction projects and historical restorations.

TWO

# Children, Young People and Labyrinths

ROSEMARY NORTON

It is a privilege to introduce labyrinths to children and young people, not least because they have an innate longing and thirst for knowing, but also because their creativity knows no bounds and they display an enormous sense of humour and fun. Children are like sponges, waiting to soak up every experience. They are adept at working with everything that is available to them when given a safe, nurturing environment that holds the boundary and provides an experience that allows for active learning – and active experience too. Working in many schools, with children from three to eighteen years, has never failed to bring to me feelings of excitement, anticipation and nervousness, and a great satisfaction that something of such depth and beauty can be so readily available to young people.

As a teacher I know that when a child has a deep experience of fun, contentment and acceptance, it lasts and becomes part of who the child is. My approach to working with labyrinths and children is thus grounded in one of respect and acceptance. I know that to be able to pass on all a labyrinth journey has to offer is always a wonderful privilege. This is not to say rigorous and clear planning is not needed. I recognise that the comprehensible organisation of the day depends on being able to hold together spontaneity and structure. Over the years I have become more comfortable at discerning what might best work with each setting and its requirements. I hope to share as much of this as I can in this chapter.

My work engages me with children and students in primary, secondary and tertiary education in the UK. I use a portable polyvinyl labyrinth imprinted with the design of the medieval labyrinth in Chartres Cathedral.

Labyrinths can be used with children in many areas of the curriculum (for example, at transition points when children move from primary to secondary school). However, my particular interest is in supporting children through their spiritual development in schools that reflect the importance of the child's faith journey as part of the curriculum. My usual, though not only, starting point when working with children is taken from the

Roman Catholic tradition, which follows the children's faith journey within the liturgical calendar.

## Structuring the day – for seven- to eleven-year-olds

At the planning stage of any school event, I place emphasis on creating an occasion lasting a whole day. My aim is to help the children to understand the labyrinth and, I hope, to have a deep and meaningful experience.

The first session explains what a labyrinth is and what is going to happen over the day. I then engage the children by inviting them to draw a three-circuit classical labyrinth. Children of all abilities enjoy drawing labyrinths and once they understand the process are able to experiment with their own shapes. For children who like a challenge there can be open-ended questions such as *'How would you make a labyrinth with more circuits?'* In posing an open-ended question there is opportunity for children to explore and express their own ideas and views without the risk of their feeling that there is a standard answer to be found and reducing the possibility of 'getting it wrong'.

I then take the creative process further by getting the children to work with clay. I have various cookie cutters for different times in the year, e.g. bauble shapes at Christmas and an egg shape for Easter. I particularly like the one that is in the shape of a footprint, a fantastic symbol and a reminder of the labyrinth day.

In my experience children have a sense of their own journey and its direction and I have found it is not usually difficult for a child to think of a 'seed word' that they find meaningful. When a child thinks about the experience they would like to have, such as peace, joy, fun, they can focus on the word during the preparation and walk. This allows each child to be more present to their experience.

By decorating their footprint or clay decoration there is a grounding in the purpose of walking the labyrinth, a reason for walking and anticipation that they are about to embark on a journey that is both sacred and exciting. This is not to say that children may not feel overwhelmed or initially afraid, as they can be with any new adventure or challenge, but that the whole nature of the labyrinth provides a nurturing safe place to wonder about life. Throughout the rest of the day the children are introduced to many aspects of the labyrinth including its construction, history, creativity and walking. This teaching is grounded in the context of the theme of the day such as recycling, transition, contemplative learning or grief.

## Creating the atmosphere

My portable labyrinth is large and heavy to handle and I always seek adult help ahead of the session to ensure it is laid out in time for the labyrinth walk to begin. In addition I like to involve the children as much as possible and usually ask for four children to help in the laying out and the placing of LED tea lights, mats and benches to create a setting that is awe-inspiring. This can take quite some time. The ambience is important, so soft liturgical music is played, the overhead lights are muted and the LED tea lights glow. The atmosphere creates a sacred space and children sense that this is a special experience. While the hall is being prepared, the class teacher, who has also been present and has participated in the morning session, will be reinforcing the context of the day so each child has the opportunity to have a rich experience.

In the UK, primary classes have around thirty children and this number has to be taken into account for overall timing to ensure each child gets sufficient time to do a walk. Sometimes parents are invited to accompany their child when they walk the labyrinth. This can be an incredibly moving experience for parents. Children, more often than not, are caught up with their personal experience of walking but may forget their experience quite quickly. I have found that providing activities before and after the walk, to be completed quietly, encouraging respect for the other walkers, helps to keep the afternoon flowing smoothly.

*Schoolchildren on an eleven-circuit medieval canvas labyrinth: Photo by Rosy Norton.*

## Managing the walk and activities

I provide photocopies of a black-and-white labyrinth drawing, on either A4 or A3 paper, and felt pens and crayons for children to record their experience in words or symbols, with stones to add decoration. Children have amazing energy and zest for life and often have a natural urge to rush. Although I do not want to discourage this I also have to be aware of health and safety implications.

Choosing soothing music, providing activities to complete and encouraging children to walk thoughtfully all help to manage the size of class and time available. When each child has walked it is important to allow time for each child, and the class as a whole, to reflect on the experience. Time is made to listen to any child who wants to share and for the class to talk together. Children often find that their experience of walking a labyrinth is one that provides words such as peace, calm, joy, space and happiness and also allows for the more difficult words such as sadness, loneliness, loss and pain. This all gives the class teacher opportunity to follow up the experience later in a way that is appropriate for the age of the child.

## Expanding the experience

My experience of using the portable labyrinth had initially provided a great resource to take into schools, but I found I wanted to offer a more cohesive experience. For instance, my focus was on giving children aged three to five the opportunity to just have fun with the labyrinth. For older children, seven to eleven years, a more open context was desired so that this could provide a more sensory and reflective experience.

I was also aware that in some settings space, or lack of space, is a factor that needs to be taken into account. My 10 metre (33 feet) diameter polyvinyl labyrinth usually fills the space available in a secondary school hall or gym. Primary schools are often smaller and it is essential to check the dimensions of the hall to ensure that there is going to be sufficient floor and working space.

A school in inner-city Manchester, UK, invited me to provide labyrinth workshops for all its pupils during celebrations for the bicentenary of Church of England schools. I considered this to be an ideal opportunity to introduce the building of a unique, temporary classical labyrinth for each class of three- to eleven-year-olds. As each class was responsible for choosing its theme, my role was to guide and help them to integrate their ideas to maximise the experience of the labyrinth. I supported the staff by helping them to know how to manage the walks and contextualise the classes' chosen themes.

On the day, some of the labyrinths were made outside, others in the classrooms and one laid out in the hall. Each class spent half a day constructing and walking its themed labyrinth, followed by a session where pupils and teachers reflected on their experiences together. The children in their final year at the school, preparing to move on to the high school, had a whole day with the labyrinth to explore what this time of transition meant to them. Once every class had walked and knew about labyrinths, a whole school celebration and reflection was held using a PowerPoint presentation of photographs taken of each class.

## Constructing temporary labyrinths

The creation of ceremony and ritual is part and parcel of the labyrinth and can serve to focus attention, increase creativity and engage the imagination (1). Temporary labyrinths can be constructed out of anything, so over many months I've collected pine cones, seeds, bark, shells, stones, natural crystals, cinnamon sticks and wood. I also include rich fabric materials such as chiffon and velvet and items which might resonate with stages in the life of a child growing up, such as soft toys and quirky objects. I find that dried-flower wholesalers have amazing resources that provide beauty, interest and colour. I want the children to have a sensory experience of building a labyrinth which includes individual choice, group cooperation, creativity and fun, and allows children to take ownership of their labyrinth and see that each item they place in it matters (2). My ultimate goal is to help each child to use the labyrinth in ways that reflect their individuality and personal journey; and, from my perspective as a psychotherapist, I hold dear the intention that they will find their own way to achieving a balanced healthy life and wholeness in 'their Being' (3, p48).

For the young children aged three to five years, the emphasis should be on having fun with the labyrinth; small children usually love stories that include repetition together with a mounting excitement and expectation of something about to happen. Using story as the starter provides the perfect springboard to launch the labyrinth journey for the young. For these children, the curriculum is grounded in play and exploration, so familiar toys, musical instruments, large construction toys and sand and water can be used to build a labyrinth. Working the toys imaginatively, a labyrinth can be constructed where the young can explore the journey through language, touch, sound and smell. For them the experience is in the moment.

Older children are more able to connect to a familiar story which has a message that the children relate to. It is helpful if this is integral to the curriculum. An example of this was a class of eight- to nine-year-olds who looked at recycling. They created their labyrinth from items collected from home and school, demonstrating how objects are not limited to one use. Likewise, a class of ten- to eleven-year-olds were able to think deeply about their transition to secondary (high) school and the journey they had already made through primary school. They were able to use the labyrinth to illustrate their individual and group journeys. As each child reached the centre of the labyrinth they took the opportunity to give thanks to their school while contemplating the qualities that they were taking to their next school.

## Labyrinths in secondary schools

When taking the labyrinth to a secondary school (ages eleven to sixteen or up to eighteen years) the needs are often different. When a child studies Religious Education to examination level, they may be required to know about labyrinths to meet the curriculum.

By helping older children to discover the labyrinth for themselves, I have found that they appear to appreciate its origins and this can lead them to be more responsive. In that attentiveness it would seem that their intellectual and emotional connection to the labyrinth increases and, for some, may well develop into a mirroring of life's journey: it becomes a metaphor for life.

Teenagers experience academic pressures to succeed and so any opportunity to minimise the stress caused by the demands and expectations of academic performance can be helpful. The labyrinth can serve to do this, by offering a purposeful walk, with no external pressure, which under the best of circumstances enables the young person to achieve much-needed 'breathing space'. When planning a labyrinth walk for such pupils it is important to allow sufficient time, bearing in mind the demands of the study timetable.

Walking a labyrinth that has up to eleven circuits allows for time, a place to rest, an oasis. The walk should be one that offers a pleasurable and restful experience, as well as particularly supporting those who might be feeling overwhelmed; support and sensitivity are at the heart of this facilitation.

## The labyrinth in a university

In addition to primary and secondary school pupils I also work with young adults. One of my most poignant experiences was of facilitating a labyrinth walk for university students who were studying dance at degree level. Students were invited to volunteer to sign up for the walk. After a brief introduction the labyrinth was opened for walking and very soon the students emerged, dancing and moving, deeply engaging with the labyrinth and with each other. The lecturer remarked that this level of engagement had not been seen before; a cohesion and shared transformation for all. The transformation that took place was tangible and the experience provided for a deepening in human spirit within the group. It was a most powerful and moving evening for everyone.

Having facilitated labyrinths for children and young people across a wide age range, I know that rigorous planning and organisation are essential. On a transpersonal level, in my holistic work as a psycho-spiritual Psychosynthesis counsellor (4), I ultimately trust that the labyrinth will provide exactly what is needed for each person, regardless of age, experience or ability. It provides for deep connections at a level that is appropriate and imprints the body of each young soul in a way that becomes part of their history and their being. The body always remembers these deep and significant moments and this allows for wholeness (5). Metaphorically, children need roots and wings. Roots so they can feel grounded and know where they come from and where they belong. Wings so they can fly, by becoming who they are meant to be, making decisions and choices and being fully in the world. The labyrinth fulfils this role beautifully.

### Resources

Practical considerations before getting started:

- Contact details of school, i.e. telephone, email address, name of teacher to liaise with.
- Do I need a police check? (Criminal Records Bureau, UK: www.homeoffice.gov.uk/agencies-public-bodies/crb/. Requirements will vary in different countries and may take some time to complete.)
- Size of space to work in. Will it fit your labyrinth? Will the space be booked for you beforehand?
- Number of children involved. How many children are you planning for?
- Will there be teachers and support staff available? This is an important consideration as these are the adults who work with the children each day.
- Timings of the day. When is morning and afternoon break? What time is lunch? If you intend to use the hall, is it also used by the children at lunchtime? This can affect the preparation for walking.
- Can messy activities (for example) be done in class or is there an art room that needs to be booked?

- Can you use the photocopier or do you have to bring enough copies along with you?
- Is any adult help available for unpacking and packing your car and laying out the labyrinth mat? This can be heavy work and different schools may have different health and safety policies in place.

Teaching aids:
- Cookie cutter: Pastry or biscuit cutters work well with air-dried clay.
- LED tea lights: Light-emitting diode. These tea lights are safer and more flexible for use in schools.
- Soothing music: Quiet, gentle music has a soothing effect on children and helps when they walk the labyrinth.

## References

1. Kindred, G. (2007) *Sacred Celebrations: A source book.* *www.gothicimage.co.uk*
2. *http://labyrinthsociety.org/activities-for-kids*
3. Draper, B. (2009) *Spiritual Intelligence: A new way of being*, Oxford, Lion Hudson.
4. Assagioli, R. (1999) *Psychosynthesis: A Manual of Principles and Techniques.* UK, Thorsons.
5. Houston, J. (1997) *The Search for the Beloved: Journeys in Mythology and Sacred Psychology.* USA, Tarcherbooks.com

## About the author

I gained my Diploma in Counselling at the Institute of Psychosynthesis in London, and am currently completing an MA in Psychotherapy, accredited by the United Kingdom Council for Psychotherapy (UKCP). I have over 35 years of experience in teaching children from three to sixteen years. I originally taught creative textiles with children aged eleven to sixteen and have a passion for working creatively with chiffon and machine embroidery within a spiritual context. In 1988 I began working in the Primary sector and was responsible for the teaching of Religious Education. I was a member of a working party responsible for writing the Religious Education Curriculum in the Dioceses of Salford. I became a labyrinth facilitator in 2007 after training at Chartres, France, with Veriditas. I now deliver labyrinth workshops to schools and the community and have a private psychotherapy/counselling practice in Manchester.

THREE

# Universities and Colleges

JAN SELLERS

What can labyrinths offer to students, to staff, to the whole academic community that comprises a university or college? The labyrinth has tremendous potential as a quiet, meditative resource that deepens reflection, supports well-being and fosters creativity. Its convoluted path, symbolic of life's journey, can be used to explore career journeys and choices; key moments such as transition and graduation; building confidence and developing professional identities and values. The labyrinth is an international resource, an inclusive and exploratory space. Children and young people can engage with the labyrinth in creative workshops including writing and storytelling. Students in creative disciplines will adapt the concept to their own design and vision. The labyrinth offers scope for student projects in many disciplines, and there is great potential for research (1).

The ancient history of the labyrinth and its presence in so many countries, cultures and faiths gives it a universal appeal: labyrinths are used by students and staff of all faiths and none. Events can be held within and across many disciplines and contexts: from Arts to Anthropology, from Careers to Counselling. The labyrinth is a valuable resource for student and staff development and for conferences and retreats. The wider community may get involved: one local nursery brings toddlers to visit a labyrinth regularly, and labyrinth walks form part of local festivals or celebrations.

In this chapter I will outline a variety of possibilities, all adaptable to different student or staff groups. My focus is on adults (18+) though schools may also find this of interest. I will touch briefly on the current surge of interest in labyrinths in Higher Education, provide practical examples and suggest sources of information and materials for anyone drawn to take their own steps in this fascinating journey.

Broadly speaking, there are perhaps four main approaches to working with labyrinths in an academic context. Most simply – once achieved – there may be a labyrinth permanently in place, for anyone to visit in their own time. Second, using a permanent or temporary labyrinth installation, there may be organised labyrinth walks – a programme of walks open to all, a walk for a local festival or as part of a well-being day for students and staff. Third, there may be workshops or seminars with specific themes (a creativity workshop, or one on deepening reflective practice, for example). Finally, a table-top (finger) labyrinth may be available in strategic locations, such as a Counselling Service reception area, for visitors to use.

A labyrinth is a beautiful artefact. Each of these approaches brings a beauty and quietness with it, an opportunity for contemplation, for restoration, or for (as Buddhists express it) 'self compassion': deepening self-knowledge and self-acceptance at a profound level (2).

## Finding labyrinths

Internationally, there are many labyrinths at universities and colleges, whether permanent installations or portable labyrinths. Others may have an accessible labyrinth nearby: use local knowledge, and try the intriguing World Wide Labyrinth Locator (3).

Drawing on this resource and a supplementary web search in preparation for this chapter, a (conservative) estimate in 2011 revealed some 110 labyrinths at universities and colleges across the world. While nearly 90 of these are in the USA, there are others in Austria and other German-speaking countries; in Australia; Canada; Hong Kong; India; Japan; Norway and the UK. Examples include the beautiful labyrinth at the Indian Institute of Technology Bombay, Mumbai, India; and student-led initiatives at Brescia College (Canada) and at Davidson College (USA). In the UK, there are permanent outdoor labyrinths at the Universities of Edinburgh, Kent, Nottingham and Stirling. Events using portable labyrinths, or other temporary installations, are held at a growing number of universities. In the UK, these include Anglia Ruskin; Bedfordshire; Dundee; East Anglia; Edinburgh; Kent; Lincoln; Liverpool John Moores; Staffordshire; Westminster and the

University of the Creative Arts.

Of the majority of permanent university and college labyrinths, i.e. those in the USA, most have been installed:

- As a commemoration for students or staff – often in memorial gardens;
- For pastoral and spiritual development;
- As a beautiful landscape feature.

For those fortunate enough to have a permanent labyrinth on site, students and staff may already be familiar with the labyrinth as a space for quiet reflection, a restorative and calming place to be. There are, however, many more ways in which the labyrinth may contribute to the life of an academic community, some of which are outlined below.

## Working with the labyrinth: practicalities

The following examples involve very different labyrinths, costs and participants, and are designed to give a strong sense of the possibilities almost regardless of budget. I say 'almost', because a crucial factor is staff time, including the time needed to develop experience and expertise in using this amazing resource. The cost of the actual labyrinth is less of an issue. Though a permanent labyrinth and a hand-painted canvas labyrinth can both be beautiful, other possibilities include labyrinths mown or painted on grass, and use of low-cost or free materials to create the labyrinth design (examples below). A number of published accounts explore, from different perspectives, the process of establishing labyrinth projects at universities (4-8); Veriditas is one key source of training (9).

Accessibility, particularly in relation to wheelchair users, raises interesting questions. No labyrinth is ideal for both pedestrians and wheelchair users, as the wider path needed for a wheelchair creates a less focused walk compared to the narrow path used by pedestrians. Fully paved (or temporary taped) labyrinths can be used by most people but involve many wide turns for the wheelchair user. The Canterbury Labyrinth (below) is a compromise: narrow stone path, but wide grass 'walls' level with the path, so that the wheelchair user follows the path with wheels on the grass. The construction of grass and stone is appropriate for the green slopes overlooking the city. However, this is not ideal for everyone and each organisation will find their own compromise. Maintenance is also a key issue: a labyrinth designed from the outset with low maintenance in mind is more likely to be sustainable (and is a more attractive proposition from a funding perspective).

*The Canterbury Labyrinth: Photo by Jim Higham, University of Kent.*

For setting out an indoor labyrinth, the challenge is often to find a suitable quiet space that can be cleared of furniture. If possible, take your own tape measure and measure up well in advance. Get a friend to check for accuracy! Look out for pillars, pipes, fireplaces and anything else that cannot be moved. Working with tape or other flexible materials, you can manoeuvre around obstacles to some extent, but not with a fabric labyrinth. Other things to watch out for are doors (which way do they open?), fixed lecterns and any other fixed furniture including computer stations which may be permanently wired in. On the other hand, staging that looks 'permanent' may turn out to be moveable; consult caretakers as experts.

## Example 1: A labyrinth for team development

This was a staff development day for a University's Partnership Development Office. The team has a remit for widening participation amongst school pupils, college students and adults in the local community. Following a brief introduction to the labyrinth, the team worked to create a labyrinth from scratch – an event that can be easily adapted for many student or staff team-building contexts. The main requirements are for the facilitator to be experienced in drawing (in this case) a seven-circuit, classical labyrinth design, and to know how to lay it out on the ground. Jeff Saward has kindly shared this technique: for drawing instructions and images, visit the Labyrinth Society or Labyrinthos websites (10-11). Resources are a few sacks of chicken-feed (dried corn or chopped maize), plastic scoops and some pegs and rope. Other materials can be used. Do avoid using dried bird-food when wild birds are nesting, as it can choke fledglings.

Part of the team lays out the pattern in lines of corn; others keep the scoops topped up. The facilitator chooses the site, marks out the centre of the pattern from which the labyrinth gradually emerges (coincidentally, this is called the 'seed pattern') and choreographs the whole event. It's helpful to allow plenty of time to consider the site in advance (including labyrinth size, and access for sack delivery) and to have a photographer for this enjoyable experience. Lucy Rutter, who led the event, notes:

> *The geometry of the labyrinth was of interest to our maths and science specialists. Arts lecturers were interested in the performance element of the production of a labyrinth, its temporality and its fascinating shape. All of the team members enjoyed the team-building aspect of the activity; as everybody pulled together to measure and mark out, and then fetch and carry, suddenly the beautiful shape of the labyrinth emerged from beneath them (12).*

Temporary labyrinths like this can be made by drawing on a beach, or with seaweed or leaves (13). Chalk works well on paved surfaces ('chunky' chalk is easiest to use); students love to decorate the labyrinth design! Another team activity is to paint or stencil a labyrinth pattern onto fabric using pebble or leaf images, resulting in a more durable labyrinth (8). All of these activities can be developed with children or adults.

## Example 2: Creativity

This example also starts with a seven-circuit, classical labyrinth, laid out in advance this time, the pattern 'drawn' with wide painters' tape on carpet. (Caution: tape is not suitable for all surfaces. Vinyl and carpet tiles can sometimes be pulled up rather easily!) Rope, string or wool could also be used, but take care with trip hazards. The taped labyrinth enabled us to use a room too small to accommodate our canvas labyrinth.

This was a creativity workshop for writers – novelists, journalists, poets – at the National Association for Writers in Education Conference, 2009. Designed by the author with Patricia Debney (School of English, University of Kent), the workshop began with a simple introduction to labyrinths. We then reflected on the concept of journey, of venturing into the unknown. At the entrance to the labyrinth, and at its centre, we placed small red gift bags. Each contained resources for a journey – objects to spark ideas (buttons, seeds, fragments of maps). Walkers could take these with them or not, as they chose. Participants walked the labyrinth and shared reflections on their journeys.

This simple and practical workshop could be adapted for any writing group, including students involved with projects and dissertations, or working to overcome writers' block and build confidence; and creativity workshops with adults and children, including Creative Writing students.

## Example 3: Teaching, learning, and personal and professional development

I offer here a host of suggestions, as the possibilities are so diverse. The labyrinth may be part of the curriculum in (for example) Archaeology; Architecture; Art; Construction; Horticulture and Landscape Design; Religious Studies; History or Literature. The experience of a labyrinth walk or workshop may provide an interactive and thought-provoking illustration of particular aspects of these studies. Through project or volunteer work, some university and college students have supported their local communities by designing and building a labyrinth.

Themed workshops can explore key aspects of students' development, within and across disciplines (6, 13). The reflective nature of a labyrinth workshop lends itself to many academic and developmental contexts including learning development; educational and staff development; careers and counselling; spiritual development and interfaith chaplaincy teams; recruitment, schools partnership and widening participation; health, well-being and disability support. Labyrinth events can also mark the start or finish of a particular programme of study or other key transition (4, 5).

As in the creativity workshop (above), each workshop includes an introduction that explores the theme and places the labyrinth in context for participants. A workshop on career journeys, for example, might invite students to reflect on the strengths that have brought them to this point, the challenges they need to overcome, and their aspirations for the future.

Following initial discussion, a labyrinth walk offers a time of solitude and introspection that may lead to deep insights. The workshop may close with shared reflections (offered more freely if students have the option to 'pass'; time may be needed to absorb the experience). Coursework – essays, journals, logs, online assignments – may be planned to include reflections arising from this work.

Examples of workshop topics include:

- Deepening reflection;
- Building a more confident professional voice;
- Developing a sense of professional identity;
- Exploring one's journey as a student;
- Career journeys;
- Exploring personal and professional values;
- Building creativity;
- Overcoming writer's block;
- Preparing for graduation or for entry to postgraduate study;
- Managing stress and anxiety in relation to exams.

## Example 4: The Canterbury Labyrinth, a labyrinth for everyone

The University of Kent's permanent outdoor labyrinth is called 'the Canterbury Labyrinth', located on a quiet, grassy slope with a glorious view of the ancient city and cathedral. It is part of the University's 'Creative Campus', built specifically as a teaching and learning resource (as well as a work of art and a performance space) (6, 14). This was a major project: excavation was needed to ensure that the base was stable. A level space was created, with tons of recycled limestone and other material for drainage, before the labyrinth itself was built on top. The labyrinth is near a public footpath and cycle path with nearby parking for wheelchair users. The use of quiet space is important – additional planting is planned, to give a greater sense of seclusion from the footpath.

This labyrinth is open every day of the year, and is visited by students (including seminar groups and project teams), by staff and by the wider community. This has included introductory events during the annual Canterbury Festival – a brief talk by a labyrinth facilitator, and time to walk the labyrinth and ask questions. The Counselling Service refers selected clients to walk the labyrinth between appointments, 'using it to facilitate meditation and reflection on their process of change' (7). Student initiatives have included drama, photography and Students' Union events. Visitors include groups from other universities, colleges and schools; community groups; faith groups and conference participants. The Labyrinth is there for everyone.

There are many options for outdoor labyrinths, some permanent, some temporary. Anglia Ruskin University have planted a daffodil labyrinth and a willow labyrinth, in collaborations between the Department of Education, the Chaplaincy, grounds staff and a local nature reserve (15).

## Time for restoration

A permanent labyrinth, or a temporary installation available at regular intervals, is a resource for staff and student well-being: a place for a restorative walk before, during or after work or studies. A well-being workshop using a labyrinth offers opportunities for relaxation and creativity, including time to draw labyrinths, write about the experience, and be playful: a counterbalance to the intensity and pressure of a working day. With the current emphasis on the student experience, this aspect of the labyrinth is at present one of the more powerful arguments for introduction of a labyrinth to a university or college.

Other special events can include arts and sustainability events;

chaplaincy initiatives; fundraising events (sponsored walks, candle-lit events with donations) and conferences. This feedback came from walkers at a conference labyrinth event, where we had not managed to achieve a secluded space:

> *Despite the noise of this busy environment, I truly enjoyed walking through the labyrinth. I was able to appreciate its potential for creative problem solving and relaxation. I was quite sad it had to end.*

> *A great release from built-up tiredness and worry. I feel refreshed and strengthened.*

> *Lovely peaceful experience – I didn't want to come out again!*

> *Brought me back into balance. Gradual letting go… wonderful.*

## Conclusion

The labyrinth provides a quiet, meditative experience for students and staff of all faiths and none. An outdoor labyrinth may be visited at any time, or during open hours, providing a peaceful breathing space that may be used in many ways, from mindful walking to dance. The only constraint is the need to respect other walkers. For many, a key aspect is the opportunity to take time for oneself. To become quiet, to deepen our understanding of inner quietness – and to slow down, in a culture that prioritises speed and haste and is often noisy – this is a rich opportunity, a time of respite and perhaps a time of transformation.

Labyrinth projects can start – and be sustained – as low-cost initiatives, supporting creativity, reflection, and personal and spiritual development at a deep level. Organisationally, such a project fosters student and staff well-being, and offers benefits to the wider community. Above all, the creation of a temporary or permanent labyrinth brings a quiet and beautiful space to any academic environment: a gift to share and a place to cherish.

## References

1. Rhodes, J. (2012) 'Open Call for Researchers and Discoverers', The Labyrinth Society [website], at *http://labyrinthsociety.org/research* (accessed 20.7.12)
2. Grace, F. (2011). 'Learning as a Path, not a Goal: Contemplative pedagogy – its principles and practices', in *Teaching Theology and Religion*, 14:2, April, pp99-124.
3. The World Wide Labyrinth Locator [website], The Labyrinth Society/ Veriditas, *www.labyrinthlocator.org* (accessed 20.7.12)
4. Bigard, M. (2009). 'Walking the Labyrinth: An innovative approach to Counseling Center outreach', *Journal of College Counseling*, 12:2, pp137-148.
5. Sellers, J. (2009a). 'Labyrinths in Universities and Colleges', The Labyrinth Society [website], at *http://labyrinthsociety.org/labyrinths-in-places* (accessed 20.7.12)
6. Sellers, J. (forthcoming). 'The Labyrinth: A journey of discovery', in: P. McIntosh and D. Warren (eds), *Creativity in the Classroom: Case studies in using the Arts in teaching and learning in Higher Education*, Bristol: Intellect.
7. Smith, M. (2010). 'The Canterbury Labyrinth', in *AUCC Journal* (Association for University and College Counselling), May, pp8-11.
8. Walker, H. (2011). 'Creating a Labyrinth: A personal and professional journey', in *AUCC Journal* (Association for University and College Counselling), March, pp20-23.
9. Veriditas: *www.veriditas.org* (accessed 20.7.12)
10. The Labyrinth Society: *http://labyrinthsociety.org* For drawing, see *http://labyrinthsociety.org/make-a-labyrinth* (accessed 20.7.12)
11. Saward, J. and Saward, K. (Labyrinthos): *www.labyrinthos.net* For drawing instructions including the chicken-feed labyrinth, see *www.labyrinthos.net/layout.html* (accessed 20.7.12)
12. Rutter, L. (2011). University of Kent; personal communication.
13. Sellers, J. (2009b). 'Exploring the Labyrinth', in *Educational Developments*, Staff and Educational Development Association, 10:1, Feb-

ruary, pp15-16.

14. Sellers, J. (2010). Interview in: The Labyrinth Society, *Labyrinths for our Time: Places of refuge in a hectic world* [DVD]. *www.labyrinthsociety.org*

15. Holley, D. (2012). 'A Labyrinth for the Chelmer Valley Nature Reserve' [online news bulletin]. At: *www.anglia.ac.uk/ruskin/en/home/faculties/fhsce/news-events/ news/archive/labyrinth.html* (accessed 20.7.12)

16. The Chantraine Dance of Expression: *www.chantrainedance.co.uk/* (accessed 20.7.12)

## About the author

Dr Jan Sellers has worked in Adult and Higher Education for many years, most recently at the University of Kent. In 2005 she was awarded a National Teaching Fellowship for her work, enabling the launch of a major new project. Jan built on her knowledge of student learning development, and personal experience as a dance student (16) and a Quaker, to explore themes of quietness, creativity and joy in relation to learning, discovering labyrinths as part of this journey. By 2008, the University had a thriving labyrinth project and the Canterbury Labyrinth was launched. The first Veriditas facilitator training in the UK was held at Kent in 2010. In 2012 Jan retired and now works freelance, offering labyrinth events and consultancy in different sectors. Her focus is on quietness, reflection and restoration: the spiritual as part of the everyday. *http://www.jansellers.com*

FOUR

# In Search of the
# Unattended Shadow

JIM BUCHANAN

I became aware of the classical labyrinth design as a child through my parents' ceramics. I would draw and practise my own interpretations on paper, in clay, and on the nearby beach (1). Later, as a landscape architect, I created temporary labyrinth installations in public parks for events and community celebrations. Now, as an artist, I explore the boundaries of form and material, with a particular interest in the dynamics of site-specific installations – both indoors and out.

Constructing labyrinths in public spaces is a continuation, per-haps, of the original applications of community celebration – to mark annual calendar cycles, feast days, religious reverence and maybe, deep down, survival itself. I use drawing exercises involving the classical labyrinth forms to calibrate my hand, eye, brain coordination within my artwork-making. Walking the labyrinth then extends this connection between thinking and feeling, by means of the physical act of movement. These are quite internalised activities, and I find it more and more important to introduce materials which act as conductors to new awareness, for example water and projected light.

So in my own practice the labyrinth exists on several levels, and I am drawn back and forth between them to pose new ques-tions within each new artwork. In proposing how one begins to work creatively with the labyrinth, I would offer the observation that regular walking gradually establishes a sense of the cadence, pathway design and visual pattern. When it is not possible to undertake the physical walk, then a finger walked around a drawn labyrinth helps reinforce the remembered sensations.

## Labyrinth as symbol

The use of the labyrinth as an important reference symbol is found in the work of graphic artists, painters, ceramicists, sculptors and others (2). This is often based upon the individual's decision to view the labyrinth as a sacred mandala, where it has become a represen-tation either metaphysically or spiritually of a larger concept (3).

Usually this involves a replication of the labyrinth design in its precise wholeness, with the emphasis upon the correct completion and attention to detail to satisfy the artist.

Labyrinths as personal emblems were very popular during the Middle Ages, and these were much more sophisticated than the present-day badge or logo. Often combined with a motto, they declared personal attributes such as wisdom, perseverance and sound moral judgement. For example, a copperplate engraving from Venice from 1623 shows the tree of knowledge within a garden labyrinth structure, below the motto 'Ducit Idem Deducitque' (The same leads and misleads) – possibly alluding to the labyrinth pathway or the inclusion of Ariadne's golden thread protruding from the structure's doorway (4).

In its simplest form the labyrinth can be viewed as a single meandering line, albeit one with symbolic meaning. This line, whether it depicts the path or walls, offers an immediate form to be explored through the medium of drawing. Most current drawing exercises focus on learning the structural layout; using the classical labyrinth seed pattern is the most common beginning point. However, I feel that a deeper experience can be achieved, enabling us to make a stronger connection to our intuitive level of drawing, one that establishes an ability to draw what we feel we are seeing inside the labyrinth structure. An exercise to try is as follows:

> Draw a classical three-circuit labyrinth on a large piece of paper at least A3 size, and overlay it with a transparent paper. Now trace with a large crayon what you can see, but keep repeating the drawing without stopping, maintaining a steady hand-speed. If tracing the wall pattern you will need to develop a smooth about-turn at the end of the walls; if tracing the pathway you can either turn about at the entrance to re-enter or make a complete circumnavigation of the exterior.

There are two ways to develop this exercise that I recommend.

Firstly: to undertake the above drawing with both hands simultaneously, as this can increase the depth of concentration to a meditative level. For this you will need to place two labyrinth drawings side by side, but make sure they are mirror images of each other. Ideally the left-hand labyrinth should have the first pathway entering to the left, and the right-hand labyrinth the first pathway entering to the right. Cover these with tracing paper, securing with tape. Now you are ready to draw with both hands, making sure you commence on the same spot within the two labyrinths.

Secondly: to draw whilst walking the labyrinth, as this extends the interaction of hand, eye and brain to whole-body movement. Initially it's better to use a small three-circuit labyrinth, so that the speed of walking and drawing can be closer and begin to interplay. You can do this either with paper secured to a clipboard, or with the labyrinth design encapsulated within plastic.

## Developing labyrinth practice

*For the individual:*
Firstly there can be an expansion of the drawing exercises, in media, scale and body interaction. Very large full-floor drawings engage the whole body and can record not only the labyrinth form but also the choreography of movement. This type of drawing is best undertaken on the beach, where the sand will accommodate drawing differently depending on its being hard or soft, wet or dry (1).

If this drawing system works well for you, then consider making a labyrinth drawing space in your garden. To maximise the benefit it should be done with an investment in quality, either

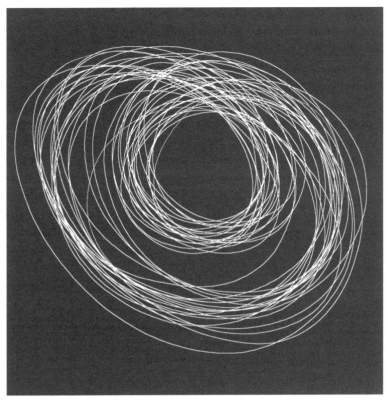

*A digital media drawing exploring the speed, balance and control of circumnavigating a seamless labyrinth walk: Image by Jim Buchanan.*

through bringing in clean new materials such as imported sand, or by preparing an area of existing ground. Soil can be dug over to remove weeds and stones, and other materials such as sand mixed in to aid workability.

The space should have a clearly defined boundary and clean materials, and if the structure is to be kept going but will be temporarily dormant, then it needs to be protected by a tarpaulin cover to keep the leaves, cats and birds off. Part of the creative process is the act of preparing the labyrinth space materials. Digging, raking, brushing and smoothing by hand warms the body and calms the mind, bringing focus and vigour into play. Working outdoors brings an added dynamic, with the weather and daily quality of light influencing what you feel and experience in labyrinth drawing.

*For your first public project:*
If you undertake regular personal drawing exercises, the fluency you develop will help you in working in more public spaces. Firstly you will have confidence in setting out the labyrinth design and guiding others in being involved. Secondly you can focus on the other aspects required of a more public scenario, such as selecting a site-specific drawing material – that is, something that might have reference to the place or people invited. For example, if working with a large group of people indoors, it is possible to use everyone's shoes to draw the labyrinth's walls. There is a wealth of other materials to choose from in making a temporary labyrinth – indeed any loosely arranged material to indicate the wall or path, such as chalk, spray paint, tape, hay, plastic cutlery, lime or sand, will do. Objects can also be laid in sequence, such as rope, shoes, plastic cutlery, tin cans, flags, sticks, boxes or bricks.

Another material consideration will depend on to what degree the labyrinth is temporary or semi-permanent. If it is to last only for a day, then the materials used need to be easily lifted, sorted and maybe re-boxed or bagged. Loose materials such as lime or sand can be easily swept up off a hard, smooth surface, but not from a grass area; however these might be left to be absorbed by the ground over the coming weeks.

Group activities within the labyrinth such as walking, running, singing and dancing can generate a lot of energy and excitement. Consider ways of 'closing down' the labyrinth at the end of an event, such as gathering everyone around the labyrinth and giving thanks. This can extend to the participants then helping to deconstruct the labyrinth and pack away the materials.

Visiting a venue in plenty of time before an event can provide answers to questions about materials and scale. In some locations a grass lawn and landowner might be conducive to making a semi-permanent turf labyrinth, or an adjacent woodland might provide sticks or leaves for a temporary labyrinth drawing (do check the weather forecast beforehand though, as you do not want windy weather when using leaves).

*Wider community projects:*
Commissions for public art projects require a certain skill-set best achieved through experience. For some artists, the hardest challenge is to apply a fluid creative process to the commissioning and construction process as these are usually large-scale outdoor installations. Requirements are likely to include preparation of instructions to builders, technical specifications, work-plans, insurance cover, and sometimes planning permission.

Since I originally trained in landscape architecture, the ability to wear a multitude of hats has been a modus operandi in my art installation projects. My key advice would be to build more time into the design and creative practice to acclimatise to the pressures of such work, and to remember that every timeline – whilst initially looking possible – invariably needs adjusting at some stage.

## Some observations on personal development

Having worked with the labyrinth for over twenty years, I begin to see the semblance of a pattern in my development. Initially there was a phase of temporary drawing projects, where the duplication of the classical seven-circuit labyrinth was a way of learning its potential applications, usually set within a landscape regeneration context, so the concept of nature cycles and rebirth was appropriate. The variable elements were in the setting, the construction materials and the way people were invited to walk the labyrinth.

Following this period came the opportunity to create large-scale installations. For example, 'Earth & Wildflower Labyrinth' in Chesterfield, constructed in 1996 (1) uses 7,000 tons of soil for the walls, creating a path length of 1.1 kilometres (three-quarters of a mile). Other large-scale works were created in Scotland, Argentina and Holland, with the latter, 'Mallem Labyrinth' (1) having a large rotunda space half recessed into the ground as the central resting place. This represented my first constructed central space with specific attributes, namely acoustics to project the spoken word and sun shadow.

The 'Mallem Labyrinth' also acted as a 'stepping stone' into a later, third phase of work; here I recently introduced a temporary camera obscura projection for the 2011 Dutch Maze & Labyrinth Symposium. The rotunda top was blocked and the small doorway had a pinhole within its centre, so creating a pitch-black interior when first entered. As one's eyes adjusted to the lower levels of illumination, a ghostly landscape view on the floor and walls became visible. This work announced my separation of the central goal from the pathway, and my focus on the centre as a meta-physical doorway to understanding nature through experience.

Of the three constituent parts of the labyrinth structure – path, wall and centre – my personal, current focus is on the central space. It represents the core for stillness, reflection, observation of how far I have travelled both physically and emotionally, and I require (some) silence and stillness to calibrate this internalised awareness. To assist this, I am happy for a while to omit the path from my personal labyrinth equation. The ongoing debate about the numerology and significance of circuits and turns I find detracts from the essence of the labyrinth experience.

## Drawing it together

My personal experience of labyrinth walking is that it can over-emphasise the introspective, and that I require an engaging phys-ical element to raise the subconscious prompts to a level at which I can remember and hold them. Simply put, I remember things better when they are connected to smells, sounds and sensations, therefore I introduce other media and objects; I find light and water the two most deeply evocative, as both are essential in supporting life – it seems a natural development in my work.

I create labyrinths of light by projecting the image of illuminated pathways using a large projector, but the walker's shadows counterbalance this with obscuration. It is this duet between dark and light, walker and shadow that engages the concentration and often reveals the unexpected. Whilst light can represent the timeless, the spiritual and the cosmos, a layer of water on the floor engages people in the physical world and anchors them in the present.

In all my projects involving water, you the walker (or swimmer) are invited to physically engage with it – either by touching it, walking through it or, in the case of the swimming pool labyrinth projections, by swimming the pathways. The key to the experience is the ritualistic act of washing oneself, maybe touching the water with the hand, stepping in barefoot, or fully immersing oneself. This adds a significant layer of trust on the part of the walker that I have created a safe environment. In return I ask for a raised level of commitment – for example by shedding one's clothes and immersing oneself in the swimming pool water (5).

By putting water and light together a dynamic alchemy begins. The water laid as a reflective floor surface will reflect all projected light and image. This is calm, still and flat until disturbed to varying degrees by the walkers' feet, offering up all manner of ripple and splash interplay. For the designer the refraction of light passing through the water adds an element of non-control to the effects. For the walker the main orientating detail is their own shadow, which alternately leads or follows them on their journey, depending on the position of light source. However the build-up of effects can lead to the reflection of both direct shadow and shadow reflection, hence you will have three shadows and two will not be connected to you.

This release of the unattended shadow represents the momentary roaming free of the subconscious, and it is this subtlety of cause and effect that inspires my creative interest in labyrinths.

## References

1. Buchanan, J. (2007) *Labyrinths for the Spirit*. London, Gaia.
2. Ewaldt, M. (2003) *Katalog Keramik und Labyrinthe*. Austria, Kultur Stadt Salzburg.
3. Tucci, G. (2003) *The Theory and Practice of the Mandala*. USA, Dover.
4. Kern, H. (2000) *Through the Labyrinth*. Prestel.
5. Rockwell, J. (2005) *Europe's Elitist Dance, Flirting Everywhere*. New York Times [website] at: *http://www.nytimes.com/2005/04/21/arts/dance/21spri.html* (accessed 20.02.2012)

## About the author

Jim Buchanan had an adventurous childhood with numerous family picnics at ancient monuments, including rolling down the Cerne Abbas Giant whilst refusing to let go of an ice cream. These experiences left an indelible impression which resurfaced later in his professional work.

Formerly trained as a landscape architect at Leeds Polytechnic, Jim explores the boundaries of form and material, with a particular interest in the dynamics of site-specific installations including labyrinths. Jim is author of *Labyrinths for the Spirit*.

Jim lives in Scotland with his family, and each year on their birthdays his boys get a garden labyrinth design corresponding to their age. *www.jimbuchananprojects.co.uk*

FIVE

# Labyrinths in Hospices

## LIZZIE HOPTHROW

Towards the end of life many people are especially aware of their spiritual needs and so the labyrinth is an ideal spiritual tool to use as an integral part of the holistic care that hospices and palliative care units offer. I discovered this when I worked as chaplain responsible for the spiritual care of patients, families and friends, staff and volunteers in Pilgrims Hospice, Canterbury (1). The hospice opened in 1982 and is one of a group of three. It serves a rural population of approximately 300,000 people and has 16 in-patient beds, a day hospice that runs a range of clinics on weekdays, and a community service. From the moment I introduced the idea of a labyrinth to a group of day patients, the Labyrinth Project took on a life of its own and was led all the way by patients. Hospices welcome people of all faiths or none (2) and so the labyrinth is particularly helpful as it contains the potential to break down any barrier of faith, culture or race.

## How it started

The first time I took a finger labyrinth (3) into the day hospice I had no preconceived idea of how to develop a labyrinth project. I had chanced upon labyrinths at Christian festivals and in Canterbury Cathedral and experienced the release from fear, the peace of heart and the inspiration and insights that a labyrinth can bring. My hope was to provide an opportunity for dying people and their bereaved loved ones to receive similar help. So I explained briefly the history and meaning of the labyrinth, using a finger labyrinth as a visual aid, before day patients were given the opportunity to make their own finger labyrinths out of clay which they could take and use at home. The response from patients was startling. Some spoke of how they had not experienced anything so spiritual before, others of how they felt much calmer when making their labyrinth, and one gentleman limped up to the labyrinth I had taken in, touched it and said 'Wow!' I was unable to understand what was happening but I *was* able to identify a call from those people who were facing the end of their lives to give them more opportunities to experience the healing potential of the labyrinth. I also discerned a call from God to discover deeper meaning in the labyrinth myself so that I could lead a labyrinth project with not only greater knowledge but also personal conviction.

## Creating a temporary labyrinth

There can be no more persuasive evidence for resources – financial and human – to be spent on a new aspect of holistic care than the witness of patients and families. Whilst finger labyrinths were appreciated, patients very quickly became dissatisfied with being unable to walk a full-size labyrinth, so at their request we explored the possibility of making a fabric labyrinth. The two possible spaces we had available were the chapel and the day hospice. Each space, with chairs removed, measured only 16ft x 14ft (4.9m x 4.3m) but although it seemed to us too small we were convinced it was right to proceed as there was such a positive energy coming from patients and the multidisciplinary team. The team all felt it was important to involve patients and carers in making it, and with some pieces of silks (4) patients, carers, staff and volunteers created colourful strips that were fixed to white cassock material to delineate the path. It became their labyrinth – involving so many people from different departments of the hospice helped to build up momentum for the project. Within Pilgrims Hospices we work with the classical design of labyrinth because it transcends all religious and cultural boundaries but is also inclusive of any religious tradition. It is also less complicated to walk, which suits the context of working with people with decreasing physical ability.

## Creating a safe haven

We began to take day patients to the chapel for group walks and were unprepared for the emotional outpourings of many of them. In its mysterious way the labyrinth drew out deep-seated hurts and sadness in a painful but cathartic way that led to inner healing for many. Groups of carers too discovered a means by which they were able to express grief and we learnt very quickly that it was important to offer a safe space for them. We provided facilitators drawn at first from the multidisciplinary team to hold the space from the outside of the labyrinth and to support walkers either emotionally or physically.

Groups of volunteers were offered opportunities to walk the labyrinth at this stage and on one occasion we learnt an important lesson. Most of them had emotional experiences which were clearly painful as the labyrinth put them in touch with their inner-most feelings. We realised that many people are, to some extent, dying inside from unresolved hurts or sadness. One volunteer who experienced a deep catharsis wrote: 'It set me on the path of finding help for myself. A great burden has been lifted and nothing has been insurmountable since.'

## Making the case for a permanent labyrinth

Patients and carers found that they benefited from the use of the labyrinth to such an extent that they began to request a permanent labyrinth – one that they could use at any time of the day or night. The fabric labyrinth could only be laid out at certain times, when there was enough help on hand to remove the furniture, to make space for the labyrinth, and to remove all the religious artifacts too, so as to provide a neutral space.

Mindful of the need to begin to build a case for a permanent labyrinth we produced a simple feedback sheet for participants. Walkers were invited to tick a list of feelings, positive and nega-tive, that they felt as a result of walking the labyrinth. Our initial findings showed 29 out of 30 people felt *calmer* having either walked or watched the labyrinth being walked on their behalf. The team believed that was strong enough evidence on which to base a proposal to present to Senior Management and Trustees.

We found that it was helpful to identify one or more members of the management, as senior as possible, who might offer support. In our organisation, we were fortunate to have two such people, one of whom requested a proposal be written, not only laying out a plan but also putting the labyrinth in a historical and cultural context. It would be likely in today's climate that a full business plan be requested which would of course raise the difficulty of spiritual caregivers being expected to measure the efficacy of their work in numbers and financial worth.

In order to foster interest in the labyrinth project, we had been involving as many members of staff and volunteers as possible. The labyrinth is still relatively unknown in the UK and it is therefore advisable to build up awareness as much as possible from the beginning, partly to educate people but also to gauge the viability and potential success of a proposed labyrinth. The response was encouraging and the process inspired an astute person to put an offer of £5000 on the table at the outset.

## Building knowledge and know-how

Naturally, it is helpful to be as knowledgeable about labyrinths and their usage as possible. Our hospice management backed an application for training with Veriditas (5) as part of Continuing Professional Development and the benefits of this training were channelled into presentations that were given to the Senior Managers. Presentations of proposals need to be visionary, realistic and based on benefits to patients, carers and the bereaved. We had no experiences of other hospices to draw on. However, the number of hospices providing either permanent or temporary labyrinths as part of their services is growing (6,7,8).

Our proposal was given the go-ahead and we discovered that a landscape gardener who specialised in building labyrinths (9) lived locally! The signs looked good. A small project group was formed to guide every aspect of the process and one of the factors that contributed to the satisfactory fulfilment of our labyrinth was excellent teamwork. We spent many hours together and with the builder deciding on the best site and the requirements of the garden, as well as the design of the labyrinth itself.

For those without a choice of site, I would suggest that sometimes anywhere is better than nowhere! We had only one viable place in the garden fit for purpose – at the front of the hospice where people could see it, yet far enough from the car park so that it could be secluded. There were two disadvantages – it was a long way from the ward and it was already a rose garden, albeit a rather ancient one. When a new labyrinth is built in a relatively large organisation, some opposition is likely and people naturally experience a sense of loss when changes are made to 'their' space. Sensitive communication is needed but also strength to protect the integrity of the project.

Our vision was to build a Therapeutic Labyrinth Garden (10) with the labyrinth as the central point of focus and secluded areas where patients, families and visitors could simply sit. Those on the Labyrinth Project Group with an interest in plants were involved in discussions with the designer and the planting plan included trees, shrubs and perennials requiring low maintenance but with all-year interest. We hoped to create a special sacred space that worked in harmony with nature and the mystery of the Spirit and so the whole garden and labyrinth was designed according to sacred geometry (9). Andrew Wiggins, the designer, wrote: 'When walking the labyrinth we are seeking unity with nature, our inner selves, spirit or God. Sacred geometry is incorporated into the design to strengthen these connections (11).'

The Pilgrims Labyrinth itself is a seven-circuit classical pattern modified to five circuits with a path wide enough for wheelchairs and mobility aids and an enlarged centre to accommodate two benches for resting and to allow wheelchairs to turn. It is made out of sandstone pavers and is designed to last for 100 years.

We had assumed it would be necessary to have that amount of width to enable wheelchairs to pass each other; however a narrower path might work just as well and would allow for either more circuits or a smaller and therefore shorter path but without

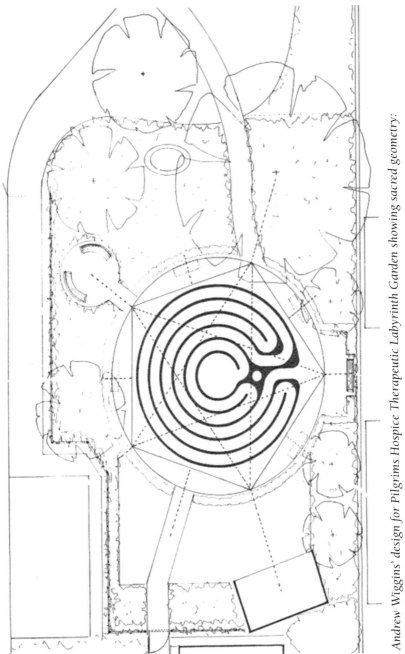

*Andrew Wiggins' design for Pilgrims Hospice Therapeutic Labyrinth Garden showing sacred geometry: andrew@labyrinthbuilders.co.uk*

compromising the smooth passage of the walk. A shorter path would be more manageable for people with impaired mobility.

Incorporated into the garden is a wooden shelter which serves as a large space for groups to gather to hear an introduction to the labyrinth or for numbers of people to meet whatever the weather. We were pleased with the plan. All we needed now was the funding!

We had the launch sum of £5000 and we hoped to attract corporate or charitable institutions to meet the shortfall, some £60,000. Soon after I had begun discussions with our corporate fundraiser, we became aware of some funding that was being made available for hospices from the Department of Health (DoH) as part of the Dignity in Care for Older People Capital Grant. When we received the application documents we discovered that this was one time we did not mind a tick-box system of assessment as we ticked them all and were granted the sum total! Pilgrims Labyrinth Garden is an expensive option in difficult financial times and I would suggest that when there are not many funds available, a simple design and fabrication is sufficient, acceptable and advisable. Nevertheless, in the UK, it would be wise to keep up to date with DoH grants for hospices.

At this stage it was important to raise awareness still further and to encourage more staff and volunteers to appreciate the benefits the labyrinth would bring potentially to the whole organisation. An artist's impression of the Therapeutic Labyrinth Garden was set up in the entrance hall along with some 'Frequently Asked Questions' (FAQs) to inform and to address misunderstandings (12). The FAQ list was also available permanently on the front desk so that receptionists would have a resource to refer to when asked about the labyrinth by visitors.

We thought it was also necessary to produce a colourful leaflet to help visitors walk the labyrinth with some understanding of its meaning and potential (13). It included some basic information, a little history of the labyrinth, some benefits with quotes from patients and carers and a section on ways of walking the labyrinth.

The leaflet was reproduced into a large weatherproof notice so that anyone approaching the labyrinth would have access to helpful information. Both the leaflet and the notice included an invitation to talk to a member of staff if painful issues had arisen. Staff are available during the day and a telephone number was included for out-of-hours contact.

## Welcoming and opening the labyrinth

We felt it was important to set the labyrinth aside as a 'sacred space' for all people to find God in their own way and so we had a Blessing Ceremony in which we laid down at the centre a piece of rose quartz to symbolise unconditional, compassionate love, distributed rose petals over the labyrinth, sang a song of blessing and played a Taizé chant. This ritual included both Christian religious and non-religious material so that all might feel included.

For our Opening Walk we invited all staff and volunteers along with some special guests including a representative from Help the Hospices (14) who had supported the project and Jeff Saward (15) who had helped to design it. Patients attending the day care unit along with their carers (family member or friend) were present and the feedback was very moving and encouraging.

One patient wrote afterwards: 'Being pushed in my wheelchair round the labyrinth by my husband, together we found it was the most spiritual and magical thing we have ever experienced. I have Motor Neurone Disease … and the feeling of inner calm and love made us both feel complete. It was thought-provoking and awe-inspiring.'

With the completion of the permanent labyrinth we were now able to take groups to walk it at any time and there were other advantages too. Patients and families could access it from the ward and we took every opportunity possible to educate ward staff so that nurses could accompany patients from the ward. Those patients who are physically limited and unable to walk or to move are still able to experience 'a walk' using a finger labyrinth. Following the death of a loved one, family members and/or close friends are also encouraged, if appropriate, to use the labyrinth as part of grief work. One bereaved relative said, 'Since walking the labyrinth over a period of time, the depression that had settled over me since my husband died has lifted.'

The way in which participants in a labyrinth walk are prepared for it may help them to receive the comfort or enlightenment they need. Working in a secular setting, we felt it was necessary to speak about the spirituality of the labyrinth in a way that included people of all faiths or none, yet made Christians feel that they could also put Jesus Christ at the centre of the labyrinth. From our experience, we learnt that the healing path of the labyrinth may begin with its introduction.

## Opening to the wider community

The organisation wanted the local community to benefit too and to that end we trained volunteer facilitators so that community groups could be welcomed and given a life-enhancing experience of the labyrinth. This also helps to break down the barriers relating to death and dying and we saw it as a mission to the local community. Church, mental health, women's and health-care professionals' groups are just some examples of those who came from the community. We had a group booking protocol but inevitably, at some time, groups and individuals would be accessing the labyrinth simultaneously and the Chief Executive Officer of the hospice raised a concern that this would cause a conflict of interests for walkers. I reassured him whilst feeling a little anxious! A typical example, however, of how we discovered that the labyrinth welcomes people with a wide variety of needs at the same time was the occasion of the Hospice Fête. There were groups walking the labyrinth with serious intention whilst others sat at the centre with their shopping and drinking beer! It looked chaotic but everyone received an experience that was appropriate for them. For most of the day and night, however, the labyrinth is free for individuals to access it quietly in their own religious, spiritual or open way.

Working in hospice and palliative care can be demanding and when there is the possibility for members of the Family Services Team to offer some formal staff support, the labyrinth fits well into this programme. On the occasions when it was used within Pilgrims, many staff found the labyrinth helped them either to find a solution to a particular problem or to let go of a variety of problems.

## Ensuring continuity and sustainability

One way of protecting a labyrinth project in the longer term is to encourage staff to work with the labyrinth routinely and to put in place practices and systems that might ensure continuation of use when there is a change of personnel. It would be wise continually to add to the evidence of benefit to patients and families so that managers may be persuaded of the desirability of the labyrinth in the unit. However, there is no guarantee that this will happen and the energy that labyrinths mysteriously contain will lie dormant until the time, the place and the people are in harmony again. The leader of the project would not necessarily need to be a chaplain, but someone with an active spiritual life and in whom some responsibility is invested by the organisation.

Lauren Artress writes: 'Walking the labyrinth … calms people in the throes of life transitions (16).' This has been our experience in the hospice and a reminder of how the labyrinth can be whatever the person needs it to be was illustrated on one of many occasions. A woman patient, who was an atheist, shortly before she died, would sit for some time at the centre of the labyrinth. She shared with her partner that it was the only place she felt calm. After she died, her partner regularly walked the labyrinth to help her deal with her grief, and in time began to experience that same peace. We have found that whether or not God's name is invoked His peace may be found within the labyrinth.

## The way forward

It wouldn't be possible to devise a strategy that would enable every hospice or palliative care centre to work with a labyrinth; however the following points are worth consideration:

- Experience the labyrinth for yourself and witness the experiences of others
- Enthuse others in your team or unit
- Visit other hospices that have a labyrinth and gain from their experience and ideas
- Begin in a small way with a fabric or finger labyrinth
- Gather a team to support you – include staff, volunteers and preferably patients
- Prepare a plan with the accent on benefit to patients to present to senior managers
- Collect feedback from patients
- Identify how funds may be raised, i.e. government bodies, charities, bequests, fundraising events
- Remember that fundraising must include repair and future upkeep of permanent labyrinths
- Hold on to your vision.

## References

1.  www.pilgrimshospices.org
2.  www.helpthehospices.org.uk
3.  Williams, D. (2011) *Labyrinth: Landscape of the Soul.* Glasgow: Wild Goose.
4.  www.vanners.com
5.  www.veriditas.org
6.  www.ayrshirehospice.org
7.  www.stmichaelshospice.org.uk
8.  www.jerseyhospicecare.com/
9.  Andrew Wiggins of The Labyrinth Builders – www.labyrinthbuilders.co.uk

10. *http://www.pilgrimshospices.org/about-pilgrims-hospices/
    publications-and-leaflet-directory/*
11. Lawlor, R. (1982) *Sacred Geometry: Philosophy and Practice*. New
    York, Thames & Hudson.
12. Hopthrow, L. (2009) *Pilgrims' Journey through the Labyrinth: A guide
    to using labyrinths in spiritual care*. Pilgrims Hospices
13. *www.pilgrimshospices.org/labyrinth/*
14. *www.helpthehospices.org.uk*
15. Jeff Saward, historian and author – *www.labyrinthos.net*
16. Artress, L (1995: Updated 2006) *Walking a Sacred Path: Rediscov-
    ering the Labyrinth as a Spiritual Practice*. USA, Riverhead Books.

## Resources

CDs:
*On the Path* by David Blonski – Timeless Productions USA
*Walking the Labyrinth* by Martin Gregory, piano – Martin Gregory
*Chartres – The Path of the Soul* – recorded live at a labyrinth walk –
Catherine Braslavsky Ensemble – ancient and contemporary sacred
music
*Soul Songs of the Labyrinth* – Lisa Rafel – recorded in Grace Cathedral,
San Francisco
Taizé chants
Margaret Rizza chants – Kevin Mayhew
Meditation music from the Brahma Kumaris World Spiritual University
– such as *Magic Lake* and *The Hidden Valley* – Eyesee
*www.bkpublications.com*
*Blessings to You* by Tami Briggs – Musical Reflections Inc.
*Calm as the Night* by Tami Briggs – Musical Reflections Inc.
*Alina* by Arvo Pärt – ECM Records
*Devi* by Chloe Goodchild – Raven Recording
*Tibet: Nada Himalaya (2)* by Deuter – New Earth Records
Chants from *Sounds of the Eternal* by J. Philip Newell – Sounds of the
Eternal

About the author

Revd Lizzie Hopthrow is an Anglican ordained priest and was Chaplain to Pilgrims Hospice, Canterbury for ten years. Her book, *Pilgrims Journey through the Labyrinth, A Guide to Using Labyrinths in Spiritual Care* was published in 2009 and was the result of her experience of initiating a labyrinth project. Lizzie's work and her book have been featured in the *Financial Times* Colour Supplement and she has been published by the *Journal of Healthcare Chaplaincy* and *Help the Hospices Information Bulletin*. In 2008 she presented a labyrinth poster at the Help the Hospices Biennial International Conference. Since leaving the hospice Lizzie works as a freelance Retreat Director and continues to teach and give labyrinth workshops at conferences and in hospices and in her own retreat garden, The Quiet View, where she also leads Quiet Days. *www.quietview.co.uk*

# Churches, Retreats and Spirituality Centres

DI WILLIAMS

The labyrinth has a long history of use as a spiritual resource. This ancient archetypal pattern is found in many different settings worldwide, including in the writings, art, buildings and spiritual practices of religious or spiritual traditions. It is increasingly an inclusive path for all faiths and none (1).

Over half the labyrinths identified in the World Wide Labyrinth Locator occur specifically in the context of religion and spirituality (2). Many, though not all of these, exist within the Christian tradition. We are witnessing a resurgence of labyrinth creation and labyrinth walking in present-day churches, cathedrals, chaplaincies, and retreat and spirituality centres. The majority of these labyrinths are in the Americas. A growing number are in Australasia, Asia, Africa and Europe. Over 75 are in the UK. Of these around 40 are in churches, cathedrals and chaplaincies. The remainder are found in retreat and spirituality centres.

It seems that many people today are looking for deep, holistic, nurturing ways of exploring, understanding and expressing their authentic spiritual experience; ways which serve to align their belief with a fresh appreciation of humanity's intimate relationship to all planetary life, to the universe, to mystery and to the Sacred (3). Within the various traditions of the church in the UK this exploration of authentic spirituality is finding expression in new interpretations of monasticism, in environmental concern for creation, in creative appreciations of being Church (for example, 'Emerging Church' and 'Fresh Expressions') and in renewed interest in the practice of contemplative and embodied prayer, spiritual accompaniment, retreats and pilgrimage (4).

It is in this context that walking the labyrinth as a spiritual practice is emerging as an ancient yet contemporary and unique resource for the engagement of the whole self – body, mind and spirit.

In this chapter I will look at this growing phenomenon in churches and retreat and spirituality centres in the UK. I will describe some examples (from England and Scotland) of labyrinth events in these contexts, including information about the type of labyrinth in use and some of the issues regarding starting, sustaining and learning from a labyrinth project.

## Featuring labyrinths

Labyrinths feature in churches and retreat and spirituality centres in a variety of ways. The most popular example is that of a simple open walk. Here the walker chooses their own time to walk either a permanent labyrinth or a portable labyrinth laid out for a publicised period (and usually facilitated). Increasingly, a led session, workshop or quiet day provides a more structured opportunity to experience a labyrinth as part of a programme of reflective learning. Churches and retreat centres are seeing the value of bringing in an experienced labyrinth facilitator or trainer to offer a range of possibilities: for example, sessions on the history and origins of labyrinths, making a crafted finger labyrinth for personal reflection, creating a temporary labyrinth to walk as a group or offering spiritual reflections or talks as part of a themed labyrinth programme.

In churches and retreat and spirituality centres there is an increasing call for consultancy and training with an external labyrinth professional. This is particularly helpful for those engaged in the early stages of a project to construct a permanent (and often costly) labyrinth, as well as for groups and institutions wishing to start a new labyrinth project or develop and deepen their current work.

## Garden Cottage Spirituality Centre Quiet Day

This event was part of Garden Cottage Spirituality Centre's yearly programme of workshops, quiet days and retreats (5). The permanent six-circuit medieval labyrinth in the centre's grounds was originally built with the generosity of supporters of Garden Cottage via a range of fundraising events. A local garden designer constructed the path from simple pavers laid into grass 'fields'. The labyrinth was built for easy maintenance with ongoing care covered by the budget for garden upkeep.

The permanent labyrinth is used regularly as a place for people coming to Garden Cottage for spiritual direction or retreat days to slow down, move into their own centre and allow space for reflection and stillness. For the Quiet Day event I deemed it necessary to lay a larger, indoor labyrinth to enable the gathered group to enjoy both a spacious walk and a deepening of labyrinth experience.

The event was open to all. This meant that the participant group had varied experience of labyrinths and labyrinth walking. The day began by sharing something of those experiences. We moved through a teaching session on labyrinths, a time of preparation for walking the indoor labyrinth, a period of silence which included a reflection on the theme of the day and a labyrinth walk. The afternoon session offered a variety of opportunities to deepen the experience of the morning, including space to walk the outdoor labyrinth.

> 'Wonderful experience, would like to learn and practise more.'

> 'The information was infused by spirituality, enthusiasm, conviction. Highly respectful of individuals taking part ...'

> 'Beautiful, wonderful, peaceful setting. Lovely lunch – kindness everywhere.'

Garden Cottage is developing its labyrinth ministry. The centre recognises that offering a range of creative events using the labyrinth will better meet the needs of different groups. For example, a winter evening outdoor labyrinth walk lit by strings of lights attracted a slightly younger constituency, with forty per cent of the participants under forty; six of these in their twenties. Half the group were new to walking the labyrinth.

## Building a retreat centre labyrinth

A group of nine staff and students from a feminist spirituality retreat group at the University of Edinburgh Chaplaincy spent a weekend constructing a 29ft (8.8m) classical seven-circuit labyrinth at Scargill House, a retreat and conference centre. It had long been my personal desire to build a labyrinth at Scargill, a place where I had lived for some years as a member of the intentional community running the centre.

On the evening of our arrival at Scargill the group spent some time walking the site and confirming the positioning of the labyrinth ready for the build the following day. The next morning the whole group was involved in laying out the skeleton of the pattern in measured cane and string. Then the 'fields' of the labyrinth were laid lightly with sports field spray paint. After a break for hot drinks it was time to place the six hundred pieces of limestone, prepared beforehand for us by the community, on the painted 'fields'. Each person picked up a stone from the pile and positioned it where they felt it would sit well on the labyrinth. For the next hour the group hardly spoke. Quite silently the stones were laid and the labyrinth emerged.

That afternoon the group dispersed to do different things. One person wrote a Gaelic blessing and one a song. Others took the opportunity to walk the new labyrinth alone. In the early evening the group went back to the labyrinth for their first walk together. As each person entered the labyrinth the rest of the group stood around the circle quietly singing and holding the space. One at a time each person walked the labyrinth alone, yet held in spirit by the group. On our final morning I led a simple processional dance through the labyrinth. The writer of the blessing read it out loud and the new song concluded the ritual space. To celebrate the building of the beautiful Scargill Labyrinth, members of the Scargill Community and members of a parish staying at Scargill were invited to walk the path.

The build was a lovely weaving of chaplaincy, church and

*Scargill Labyrinth: a classical seven-circuit labyrinth created by staff and students from the University of Edinburgh: Photo by Di Williams.*

retreat centre experience. It offered significant learning and group development for the university team in working collaboratively, experiencing labyrinth construction, and facilitating a first labyrinth walk for a church group. In return, Scargill House received a gift of a permanent labyrinth for the ongoing use of the community and guests (6).

Subsequently the author has led both a weekend labyrinth retreat and a Veriditas Pre-Qualifying Workshop & Labyrinth Facilitator Training weekend at Scargill using the outdoor Scargill Labyrinth as well as a portable indoor eleven-circuit medieval labyrinth (7).

## Open walk – Holy Trinity Church, Melrose

Holy Trinity began their labyrinth project in 2010 with the creation of a portable seven-circuit classical labyrinth made from canvas (8). A member of the church, enthused by the labyrinth project at the University of Edinburgh, worked with the Rector and two other church members over the course of a day to glue the lengths of canvas together, draw out the design and then paint the canvas. The canvas was designed to fit spaces in both the church and church hall. In the church this entailed the removal of three pews from the back rows of the nave which were then repositioned around the walls of the west end to create a quiet, reflective space for the labyrinth. The total cost of preparing the nave, making the labyrinth and designing publicity was around £800. Advertising is the main ongoing cost. Staffing of events is by trained volunteers.

In December 2011 the local press wrote about a series of six open walks taking place in the church in the lead-up to Christmas. The space was well prepared. The labyrinth lay in subdued light surrounded by candles. Incense and soft music helped create a tranquil atmosphere. Volunteers offered visitors a hot drink and warm socks for walking the labyrinth and directed attention to the prepared information leaflet and labyrinth books. There was a comment book available for those who wished to write a reflection after their walk. Prayer requests could be left. It was also possible for anyone to speak in private to one of the volunteers staffing the labyrinth event.

The open walks were advertised as 'a reflective space in the midst of the busy Christmas season'. The church was keen that this nourishing resource should be offered to the wider community, not just their own congregation (9). According to the Rector and volunteers around forty people walked the labyrinth over the six days. These were predominantly non-church people. Although many were unused to participating in religious events, for them the labyrinth became a path of welcome to explore their spiritual journey.

A walker writing in the comment book said:

> 'The peacefulness and quiet nurturing energy of the church lends itself to this meditation. Being given a space for quiet reflection … is a beautiful gift which I thank you for. The music and incense, a delight to the senses, helped transport me to a quiet place of reflection.'

The church is now thinking of other times in the year to offer open labyrinth walks. In terms of the sustainability of the project, the creation of a more permanent labyrinth in the west end of the nave may be a future possibility. There is also some interest in exploring a possible collaboration with the nearby hospital in funding and building a labyrinth project there.

## Emmaus House Retreat staff training, Edinburgh

This was a three-hour session offering training to a retreat house community (10). The community had recently built a labyrinth in the small back garden of the house with the help of a landscape designer. He led them over two weekends in clearing and preparing the ground, bringing in two tons of gravel and laying the stepping stones which mark the path. Medicinal, culinary and biblical herbs were planted later in the corners of the garden around the labyrinth. At the time of this training event, the Emmaus House website already featured a labyrinth page suggesting

> In the fast-paced world in which we now live, we need simple, beautiful places like labyrinths that draw us in by the attention of their pattern to slow ourselves down, still the busy mind and connect us again with our deep inner resources (11:21).

and revealing a genuine hope that

*… visitors to Emmaus House will find in the labyrinth
just such a place of stillness at the very heart of the city
(12).*

With the labyrinth already a significant facility, regularly being
walked by guests, the community now wanted to develop their own
knowledge and understanding and do some personal and group
reflection on how they could better present the labyrinth to those
who visited the centre and deepen their own spiritual practice.

The session began with a sharing of each person's experience
of walking labyrinths and the significance of that experience to
their own story. The author ascertained what each person wished
to gain from the training session and suggested what was possible
to cover in the three hours.

After a focused presentation on labyrinths there was an open
period for questions and discussion with a clear focus on issues
regarding the use of the labyrinth in the life and work of retreat
and spirituality centres (13).

The rest of the morning was given to introducing a labyrinth
walk and experiencing a group walk together, followed by a time
to process the walk both personally and in relation to the ministry of Emmaus House. The group were encouraged to write
down their reflections. The session concluded with an opportunity
to feed back something of the experience of the morning. Discussion continued over lunch.

One issue that came up in the feedback session was how deeply
the group had engaged with the walk. For one person it had given
internal space for an issue of deep distress to emerge into the con-
scious mind. This was a timely reminder that walks in a context of
training demand as attentive facilitation as in any other situation.

Other feedback topics included how to help guests 'experience
their experience', trusting rather than over-analysing. Also, how to
help guests process their experience with appropriate support.
Further comments concerned the importance of an outdoor
labyrinth in an urban setting, creating a labyrinth leaflet for guests

to read before walking, signage round the labyrinth to help with maintaining a silent space, and introducing finger labyrinths.

## Labyrinths for 'all faiths and none'

In 2009 I co-led a multifaith team of staff and students from the University of Edinburgh who had been accepted to lead two sessions at the Parliament of the World's Religions in Melbourne. Our Chaplaincy delegation included a Buddhist, three Christians (spanning conservative, progressive and Spiritualist communities), a Hindu, a Muslim and a Shaman. We were, in our diversity, a microcosm of the Parliament gathering. We offered a documentary film, in which the labyrinth featured, and a guided labyrinth walk as one of the times of spiritual observance in the Parliament (14). People from many traditions walked the path that morning. As walking the labyrinth is a process rather than a doctrinal narrative it allowed for each person to remain true to their own spiritual integrity. Walking the path together became an open-hearted motif of the earth community's faiths.

This experience deepened my understanding that labyrinths are welcome paths for all. My sense is that some retreat and spirituality centres, chaplaincies and even churches are becoming more open to this generosity of approach. In multifaith contexts it is helpful to prepare an appropriately worded information leaflet. It also helps to include images or quotes from varying traditions in session or workshop material. The signage at the entrance to the Edinburgh Labyrinth includes the words:

> 'The Edinburgh Labyrinth is a path of welcome for those of all faiths and none.'

This recognises and celebrates the inclusive nature of labyrinths (15).

## Conclusion

The benefit to churches and retreat and spirituality centres in developing work with the labyrinth is significant. A labyrinth offers a gracious container for quiet reflection and discernment, for ritual and celebration, for contemplation and trust, for connection, growth and healing (16). A labyrinth project can support the pastoral care, mission and spiritual life of a community, nurturing all ages and a diversity of backgrounds. It is an ancient yet new practice for the soul's nourishment; a sacred gift for the 21$^{st}$ century.

## References

1. Williams, D. (2012). 'Labyrinth of the Soul', in *Faith Initiative: Embracing Diversity*, Issue 26, pp24-25.
2. World Wide Labyrinth Locator: *www.labyrinthlocator.org*
3. Woodhead, L. (2012). 'The quiet revolution in UK faith', in *Church Times*, 10.02.12, p12.
4. Simpson, R. (2011). 'Leaving the Shore', in *Retreats 2011*. No 190, pp14-16.
5. Garden Cottage Spirituality Centre, Kilgraston, UK: *www.gardencottagespirituality.org.uk*
6. Scargill Movement, Kettlewell, UK: *www.scargillmovement.org*
7. Veriditas (UK Workshops & Facilitator Training): *www.veriditas.org*
8. Holy Trinity Episcopal Church, Melrose, UK: *http://www.holytrinitymelrose.org.uk*
9. Geoffrion, J.K.H. 'Labyrinths in Churches', The Labyrinth Society [website], at *http://labyrinthsociety.org/labyrinths-in-places* : (accessed 08.02.12)
10. Emmaus House Retreat Centre, Edinburgh, UK: *http://www.emmaushouse-edinburgh.co.uk*
11. Williams, D. (2011). *Labyrinth: Landscape of the Soul*. Glasgow: Wild Goose.
12. Bain, A. (2011) 'Labyrinth at Emmaus', Emmaus House [website] at *http://www.emmaushouse-edinburgh.co.uk*

13. 'Labyrinths in Retreat Settings', The Labyrinth Society [website] at *http://labyrinthsociety.org/labyrinths-in-places* (accessed 08.02.12)
14. 'All We've Got': Film, Part 1, *http://youtube/a938yuKzCqA*: Part 2, *http://www.youtube.com/watch?v=lODnVJrdqoQ* (labyrinth 3.48-4.40 minutes)
15. Edinburgh Labyrinth: *www.labyrinth.ed.ac.uk*
16. Williams, D. (2013), 'The Healing Path of the Labyrinth', in *Retreats 2013*, no 192

## Resources

World Wide Labyrinth Locator: *www.labyrinthlocator.org*
Emerging Church, UK:
*www.emergingchurch.info/research/jonnybaker/index.htm*
The Labyrinth Society: *www.labyrinthsociety.org*
The Retreat Association: *www.retreats.org.uk*
Still Paths – a labyrinth resource and consultancy: *www.diwilliams.com*

## About the author

Rev Di Williams MBE, MA is an Anglican priest and founder of Still Paths, a UK-based labyrinth resource and consultancy. Her background is in secondary, tertiary and adult education.

She is a freelance labyrinth creator, consultant, advanced facilitator, and the UK Master Teacher for professional labyrinth facilitator training. Di is particularly experienced in working with labyrinths in higher education, retreat and spirituality centres, churches, movement-based healing arts, and children's and young people's groups. She guides people from all sorts of backgrounds in deepening their reflection and discovering wisdom for walking their unique path in life. One of the gifts she brings to labyrinth work is a deep appreciation of physical, emotional, intellectual and spiritual connection.

Di received the MBE for Services to Higher Education for leading work in multifaith and spiritual support. She is the author of *Labyrinth: Landscape of the Soul* (2011). Glasgow: Wild Goose.
Still Paths: *www.diwilliams.com*

# Community and Public Labyrinths

## DAVID KELF

## A case study – the Seaton Labyrinth, East Devon

This chapter is based on my own experiences and those of others when we built the community labyrinth in Cliff Gardens at Seaton, Devon, UK in 2005. I hope it will give some insight into the construction and use of a labyrinth for public pleasure and education, as well as for spiritual and therapeutic benefit.

Seaton labyrinth is laid out in an eleven-circuit medieval design measuring 60 feet (18 metres) across with element-toughened grass pathways and Jurassic Coast stone divides. It has a scaled oak-carved finger labyrinth and information board near its entrance.

## In the beginning

The idea can be traced back to the experience I had in the early 1990s when I encountered the little seven-circuit labyrinth at Schumacher College in Devon and, a few years later, when members of the Axmouth-based Spiral Centre healing group (1) visited the labyrinth at Chartres Cathedral. It wasn't until 2003, however, that several of us realised we had been holding a possible candidate project to celebrate Seaton Town's own millennium – the one thousand year anniversary of the granting of the first town charter in 1005 AD. After many meetings and discussions the labyrinth idea, amongst others, was approved. Seaton Town Council became the first to financially commit to the project, followed by other local and national funders, with a target date of July 2005 set for completion.

It was decided to raise awareness of the project in the local community and a well-attended talk and meditation experience, based on her book *Walking the Labyrinth*, was given by Tchenka Jane Sunderland (2). This raised the level of local interest and, I am sure, inspired later participation by residents from the Seaton and district community. Key personnel needed to further the project were identified and approached for their support. Without exception this was forthcoming.

*Seaton Labyrinth: Photo by Joy White.*

A site known as 'Cliff Field' was chosen, permissions were obtained and restrictions were identified on what is a public cliff-top recreational, but previously under-used, park, e.g. nothing more than ten feet high (three metres) to be constructed and within existing paths and access points. A close connection with the newly designated Jurassic Coast World Heritage Site (3) was intentionally included from the start.

Without this general community support and approval, as well as the involvement of several established community groups in Seaton and Axmouth, it is doubtful whether the project could have maintained the necessary momentum. At all stages, though, it never once felt like we would not succeed; this is always a good guide as to the viability of a project.

Other potential labyrinth-builders should bear this factor in mind. It can take a considerable time to 'prepare the ground'. It is time well spent. Patience is often needed but this period is necessary and worthwhile in order to establish a strong foundation for a project. From start to finish the whole project took about two years.

## Purpose and design

Apart from celebrating Seaton's history the main purpose was, and still is, to provide an interesting public amenity linked to the adjacent natural Jurassic Coast World Heritage Site; one which offers metaphorical and metaphysical insights into the personal journey through life as well as other spiritual, therapeutic and enjoyable outdoor experiences. It was intended that everyone should feel welcome to participate in the labyrinth experience at any time.

Several months were spent forming a core group at the local adult Education Centre. In an organic way, and with the help of others, notably Tchenka Jane Sunderland, photographer Joy White (4), contractor Tony Benger (5) and sculptor Michael Fairfax (6), it was agreed to combine the designs from the medieval labyrinth at Saffron Walden (7) and the labyrinth at Chartres. Discussion took place over how the labyrinth should be constructed and the nature of the pathways but eventually it was considered preferable to use the existing element-toughened grass and to divide the pathways by 6-inch-wide (15 cm) lines of stones from quarries along the whole length of the Jurassic Coast.

By walking along the designated coast one experiences 185 million years of evolution in about 100 miles. By laying circuits of stones covering this time period to define the labyrinth, as shown on the site interpretation board, we were very pleased to link the labyrinth with the official aphorism of the Jurassic Coast, which is 'A Walk Through Time' – in our case within just a 60 feet (18 metres) diameter circle.

A further connection with our own evolutionary story was provided by including a large spiral ammonite fossil at the centre of each of the four lobes (SE, NE, NW and SW) and a smoothed circular slab of Portland stone, showing myriads of small fossils, at the labyrinth centre.

Finally an accurate, scaled drawing of the proposal was produced from which building work could commence.

Because the available space limited us to 16 inch (41 cm) wide pathways for an eleven-circuit labyrinth, also included in the design was a carved finger labyrinth, positioned in front of the main labyrinth on a pedestal suitable for use by partially sighted, blind or otherwise disabled persons. This was made by well-known local sculptor Michael Fairfax (6) from a beautiful piece of local oak.

The main interpretation board itself also required careful design, on similar lines to other Jurassic Coast boards, and this was done in conjunction with staff based at Dorset County Council who eventually produced it.

The process of community involvement included sessions with wheelchair users, local councils, designers and others. Through this direct participation, the design work helped to firmly cement the idea, and a sense of ownership, in local minds. All this was coordinated by enthusiastic volunteers.

## Funding

Contractors' estimates and choosing the appropriate balance of volunteer, community service and paid labour aided the process of calculating a costing with which to approach potential funders. There were several relatively small funders, the main one being the Local Heritage Initiative (LHI) (8). The first costing was a sizeable underestimate, due mainly to the unexpected time and cost of labour to hand-lay the stones, but this was updated and approved by the LHI as we went along. Additionally we had to cost the peripheral support items, i.e. the finger labyrinth, the guide leaflet, the adjacent seats, the interpretation board, the official project photographs, the access pathway work, the time capsule, the postcards, the education pack, specialist advice and the special stones. All of these are important in supporting the labyrinth aesthetic and the experience itself. The final total cost was around £25,000.

## Building the labyrinth

The labyrinth was positioned by dowsing for the central energy point, then the whole pattern was transferred from the drawing to the ground (9). It was marked out by the local football club linesman and the channels, about 6 inches wide (15 cm) and 6 inches deep, were cut and filled with the appropriate cemented stones from different coastal quarries.

It had been a considerable job to source, and have the British Geological Survey approve (10), all the required stones and to bring them to Seaton. The channels for the stones were cut and dug by volunteers, contractors, community service people and members of a local home for the disadvantaged. It was a big job. I remember one of the contractors being amazed when the final cutting joined exactly with the first! We raised a glass to Ann Pengelly, our expert in technical drawing (11).

Laying the stones and positioning the ammonites was undertaken and care was taken over the consistency of the mortar mix to set the stones. This is vulnerable to the ever-changing weather conditions, especially when in contact with the ground, and this has been an ongoing maintenance problem since.

After the main construction was complete the two entrance stones from the quarry at the village of Beer were added. These stones were cut by hand and made a significant difference to the 'feel' of the labyrinth. It seemed right to include stones from the local quarry especially as this has in the past, famously, provided stone for many well-known buildings, including Exeter Cathedral (12). These are the 'Gateway' stones.

The labyrinth took about four months to build, exceeding the original plans and doubling the original estimated cost of labour.

However, after an informal ceremonial walk one lovely spring evening by over thirty people linked by Tibetan prayer flags, all was ready for the opening event exactly on time. The public opening ceremony, led by David Shreeve, Director of The Conservation Foundation, took place in July 2005. Witnessed by hundreds of local people, the centre stone was laid over the time capsule and speeches were made.

## How the labyrinth is being used

Since its construction the labyrinth has been attracting people who come out of curiosity, while others are brought by the need to resolve, through reflective meditation, some personal difficulty or challenge. Groups of schoolchildren have made organised visits, and other local people bring visiting family and friends. Others have simply stumbled on it by chance. It also has its enduring devotees.

The labyrinth is used by local groups including The Spiral Centre (1), which offers full-moon walks regardless of weather, often by the soft light of the moon rising over the sea. Attendees at this walk process in a well-spaced, unpressurised line but join together around the centre stone to form first an inward contemplative circle and then an outward-looking group peering upwards towards the starry heavens. This manifests an unseen connection between Cosmos and Earth that can be felt as a participative action of synthesis between the realms. Sometimes, but not always, reference is made to the Lucis Trust astrological pamphlets on full-moon meditations (13).

When many people walk the labyrinth at the same time it seems to bring the labyrinth itself to life – as it pulses with an ever-changing pattern of relationships between the participants. It is strikingly symbolic of how we interface with each other throughout our lives and sheds light, and powerful perspective, on our own unfolding journeys.

Whether people walk with expectation, wishes, prayers,

intentions, or just let go to whatever feelings arise, it matters not. There are no rules other than to be respectful to the labyrinth and to other users. Sometimes it is an experience of communion with the elements, other times fresh inspirations or insights arise naturally. Sometimes it is just a good walk with one's own thoughts or even none at all – an emotional and spiritual emptying.

## Learning from the experience

There have never been any staff attached to the Seaton labyrinth, and although many people have brought and shared their whole life's experience and knowledge for the benefit of others, no formal training has ever taken place. People have learned a lot about labyrinths simply by using it and by meeting others who are interested, then sharing information and experiences. All sorts of folk arrive and all sorts of life-changing stories are related.

As part of the funding package the LHI required us to produce an 'education pack' and parts of this are available on CD from The Spiral Centre or by contacting myself.

*Establishing the labyrinth:*
From the very start many community and Spiral Centre events have been held at, or in relation to, the labyrinth. All have helped to establish the labyrinth in the minds of many people.

*Ongoing maintenance and funding:*
Seven years on from construction the labyrinth is a valued part of Seaton's scene. Seaton Council agreed to take responsibility for the labyrinth for the first three years, while The Spiral Centre still cherishes it and continues to contribute as much as possible, both financially and practically, to its care, maintenance and usage. The task, and cost, of ongoing maintenance should not be underestimated. Indeed it should be seriously considered at the very first design stage and this may well be the overriding factor in keeping ongoing costs, and work, to a minimum.

## Experiences and reflections

Seaton's Cliff Field is exposed to the whole range of the elements. It also provides marvellous coastal views right across Lyme Bay. Depending on the mood of the weather, as well as the inner feelings and intentions of the walker, the labyrinth walk never provides the same experience twice. There is often a strong sense of grounding with the Earth but also, at times, a definite connection with the vast and changing sky above. There must be as many individual memorable experiences as there are people who have walked the labyrinth; it is a very personal thing.

I love to see young children running around the labyrinth. They are so natural and just bathe in the pleasure of following the pattern and reaching the centre without any need to analyse it or to think why they are doing it; a lesson to us all. Older folk tend to lose this sense of freedom and I have seen some hesitate in confusion as to 'what *should* we do here'. In fact, there are no rules at all – except to follow the grass pathway with respect and give thanks for the experience, whatever it brings.

## Findings and further ideas

*Benefits*
1. A beautiful space based on the traditional therapeutic and symbolic idea of walking the pattern of life's journey.
2. A connection with the elements – water, fire, earth and air – and particularly with our home planet Gaia, its place in the cosmos and our own story of evolution.
3. An enhanced appreciation of our interconnectedness with all of nature.
4. A quiet space to listen to the messages of the heart.
5. A sharing of labyrinth experiences with others.
6. Many unexpected, creative works that have arisen directly from labyrinth experiences and inspirations.

*Difficulties*

There have been few instances of vandalism or bad behaviour but when this has occurred the main responses have been to quietly explain the significance of the labyrinth or to rectify any damage as quickly as possible. It is usually possible to bring something of the labyrinth's wide-ranging benefits and attractions to the attention and appreciation of most people.

## Conclusions

Linking a labyrinth with local heritage, education and healing, along with creative projects, will consolidate the labyrinth into the fibre of a community.

Active agreement from the local community, and involvement by all the agencies and individuals, will encourage a sense of ownership and therefore ongoing care of any public labyrinth.

Thought should be given to how a new labyrinth might be connected with the wider world of similar projects.

The Seaton labyrinth is much as originally intended. The main lesson has been to try to reduce the ongoing maintenance difficulties. These should be fully appreciated during the initial design stage and minimised as much as possible.

*Further ideas and developments:*
- To gain an understanding of energy-field changes, perhaps influenced by walkers. More ongoing research could be performed by repeated dowsing of the labyrinth area.
- More could be done to include the labyrinth in local trails.
- Organised storytelling, guided walks and educational visits for all ages have begun.
- There is an increasing interest in linked pilgrimage routes. Connecting labyrinths to these would be a very meaningful addition to cross-country footpath-walking in England.

# References

1.  The Spiral Centre. Christina Bows, Combe Farm, Axmouth, EX12 4AU
2.  Sunderland, T.J. (2004) *Walking the Labyrinth*. Self-published; copies can be obtained in the shop at Norwich Cathedral.
3.  Jurassic Coast website *www.jurassiccoast.com* then links to view map, Gateway Towns and Seaton.
4.  White, Joy at *www.blackandwhiteimages.co.uk*
5.  Benger, Tony at *www.tonybengerlandscaping.co.uk*
6.  Fairfax, Michael at *www.michaelfairfax.co.uk*
7.  Saffron Walden at *www.labyrinthos.net*
8.  Heritage Lottery Fund: *http://www.hlf.org.uk/Pages/Home.aspx*
9.  British Dowsers: *http://www.britishdowsers.org/learning/what_is_dowsing.shtml*
10. British Geological Society: *http://bgs.ac.uk/*
11. Pengelly, Ann at *www.annpengelly-stainedglass.co.uk*
12. Exeter Cathedral, Devon, *http://www.exeter-cathedral.org.uk/*
13. Lucis Trust, Twelve Spiritual Festivals: Meditation at the Full Moon, *http://www.lucistrust.org/*
14. Dealler, R. (2011) Michael and Mary Pilgrims Way, Brentor to Glastonbury. *www.marymichaelpilgrimsway.org*
15. Brian Howard, *Earth Currents and Spirit Paths* pamphlet from Old St Margarets Ruins; *bhoward@btinternet.com*

# Resources

Wensum Park Public Labyrinth, Norwich
*http://www.geograph.org.uk/photo/166480*
The Labyrinth Society's labyrinth locator is an excellent resource to find a labyrinth in your area:
*http://labyrinthlocator.com/locate-a-labyrinth*

## About the author

David Kelf is a retired meteorologist and member of the Cloud Appreciation Society. He has been active in renewable energy and educational projects. Currently he is involved with the Hopton-on-Sea St Margaret's church ruins restoration project and promoting the Michael and Mary energy lines pilgrimage route from Hopton-on-Sea to Land's End (14), (15). David can be contacted at: *dkelf@btinternet.com*

# EIGHT

# The Freedom of a Labyrinth in a Secure Setting

CATHERINE MOON

*'I felt as if I were walking in the countryside.'*

It was a June day in 2008. A group of patients gathered to prepare for their walk around the labyrinth, which was the very first walk of its kind to take place in our High Secure psychiatric hospital. As I greeted the patients, I talked to them about the labyrinth and its long and fascinating history which predates organised religion. Surrounded as we were by a tall concrete wall that encloses the grounds of our hospital, I invited the men to step into the sense of freedom that a labyrinth walk can offer. *'The path is yours to walk as you choose. The only decision you have to make is whether to enter it or not.'*

The weather was unsettled. Scudding grey clouds threatened rain but as the men stepped into the first circuit the sky began to clear and the sun beamed down. The feedback was encouraging and included:

> *'I felt very close to nature. I could hear the birds singing. The walk was full of life.'*

> *'I forgot where I was for a moment. I would have liked to walk the labyrinth in a different place.'*

> *'I could feel the warm sun on my neck. It was very peaceful.'*

> *'I really felt as if I had left the ward behind. I forgot my troubles. I looked at the blue sky. It felt very peaceful.'*

> *'I felt as if I were walking in the countryside.'*

When asked if they would journey around the labyrinth again, the response was a unanimous 'Yes!'

The garden labyrinth can now be enjoyed by patients in walking groups each week, as well as on individual walks when staff are available to accompany them. In addition to the outdoor, permanent labyrinth, we also lay down portable labyrinth canvases in the chapel which are occasionally incorporated into a service of worship for patients. Labyrinth days have been organised using both the garden and canvas labyrinths. Although I have presented a number of labyrinth workshops specifically for staff, very few use it for themselves. Currently, I am the only member on our team who arranges and facilitates labyrinth events.

Ashworth Hospital offers psychiatric care to over two hundred men in a High Secure setting (1). The average stay for treatment is seven years; about 80% are admitted via the Criminal Justice System. Following their admissions, many get well and, because they no longer need such a degree of security, their journey toward recovery and rehabilitation continues with a move to other facilities. On that day in June, Ashworth Hospital, part of Mersey Care NHS Mental Health Trust, blazed a trail. Sir David Henshaw, Chair of NHS North West, officially opened the labyrinth, commenting *'The labyrinth holds an extraordinary symbolism within an extraordinary hospital.'*

We are thought to be one of the first hospitals in this country to have established a labyrinth and certainly, at that time, were the only High Secure psychiatric hospital in the UK to have one. Indeed, it was then quite possibly the largest labyrinth in the grounds of any hospital in the UK. How did we go about this?

During the years that I lived and worked in California, Grace Cathedral in San Francisco built two large labyrinths, one inside the building and one outside on the plaza (2). The Revd Dr Lauren Artress was enormously influential in this project, having researched the subject and inspired and supported its realisation. I was ordained in Grace Cathedral and often found myself returning to its cool and beautiful space. Thus it was that the labyrinth began to become a part of my life.

When I took up my post as Anglican chaplain within Mersey Care, the path to my office, within the secure site at Ashworth Hospital, led me by a large, square area of lawn, flanked by flower beds and low bushes. Every time I walked through this space my mind wandered back to the labyrinth at Grace. I began to realise that here, within the walls of this hospital, was the perfect spot for a labyrinth. I took my idea to my manager, the Revd David Glasson, then Head of Spiritual Care. We imagined, envisioned and began to realise the particular benefits that a labyrinth would offer in the setting of our specialised mental health care. We chewed over practicalities and financial implications. We also knew that we would have to face the necessary challenges and responses from our security liaison. The labyrinth had to be safe for everyone to use and so we had to decide what sort of design would work best and also how it would be funded.

My manager and I met with personnel from the Trust's horticultural team to choose a design. It was decided to use the simple classical style. Crucial issues of security and safety dictated what we could use to line the circuits, and the decision was made to plant small box hedges to mark the pathways. The plan was presented to higher executive management. It included the rationale and support for the potential benefits to mental health and physical well-being, and funding from High Secure Services was eventually approved.

There is now a beautiful hedge-labyrinth comprising over two thousand box plants. It is approximately 70 feet (21.3 metres) in diameter with nine circuits leading to an oak tree in the centre; the walk to the centre and out again is almost a kilometre in length. The pathways are grassed and wide enough to accommodate two walkers abreast (and the lawnmower!). Grounds personnel keep the labyrinth well maintained although some of the box hedges now need replacing. At the moment there are no funds for replacements.

## Preparing the way for patients to walk the labyrinth

I knew that our patients might need guidance as they made their way around our labyrinth; but initially the question was what sort of guidance would be of most help to them. Some of our patients

*Ashworth Hospital Labyrinth: Photo courtesy of Mersey Care NHS Trust.*

find it difficult to sustain silence; others need encouragement with just the right amount of stimulation. Some of our patients have difficulty maintaining a focus and are easily distracted, while others might be helped by gentle creative input. The challenge was how to create a balance in meeting the different temperaments and needs amongst those patients who wanted to take part in a walk. We thought it might be helpful if we devised a guided walk for patients and set about selecting images and themes that had the potential to gently focus the mind. One example is a theme from nature, known as the 'Cycle of the Seasons'.

I have incorporated this theme into the many retreats I have led over the years. I believe that the seasons, with their ever-changing landscapes of colour and texture, warmth and cold, new life and death, offer a rich metaphor for our human experience. Both our inner and outer landscapes are constantly influenced by hope, renewal, loss, death and rebirth, all of which are mirrored in the cycle of the seasons. For these reasons I feel that 'walking the seasons' has a profound effect in uniting us more closely with our inner world and the rhythms of life.

In preparing the walkers, they were invited to carry with them five small laminated cards. In addition we placed coloured ribbons at points around the circuit which served as a reminder to stop and pause and ponder before walking on.

Our hope was that the cards would evoke the atmosphere of each season. For example:

Spring:
The darkness of winter gives way to longer brighter days.
Air refreshing; hope returning; new life beginning; new growth appearing.

Autumn:
The Autumn card reflects the process of time for winding down, seeking shelter and building endurance.

Winter:
Nature resting, sleeping, dying; the bareness of trees and hardness of frost; the enveloping darkness of long, cold nights. The waiting.

Summer:
Nature come to fruition; potential realised. A time of warmth and relaxation; of brightness and beauty; of fulfilment; of joy and laughter.

*Colour walk:*

Another example of a guided walk uses a small laminated card with the image of a rainbow, which encourages the walker to respond to colours as they journey.

Side one of the card invites:
- During this walk you will be guided to think about colour.
- You will find coloured feathers placed at intervals around the pathway.
- Each marks a position to pause and reflect on a colour.
- At the entrance pause and recall your favourite colour.
- To help your reflection on a particular colour some brief comments are found on the reverse of this card.
- Take your time, enter the labyrinth. Follow the path, remember you cannot get lost.
- At the first stopping place think of a colour that makes you feel energetic.
- Check the second card to see if there is a comment about this colour.
- At the second stopping place think of a colour that makes you feel angry.
- Check the second card to see if there is a comment about this colour.
- At the third stopping place think of a colour that makes you feel happy.
- Continue to the centre – pause and look at colours around you; in the sky, clouds, the buildings, the trees, grass and flowers, the bushes, the clothes you are wearing etc. Focus on a colour that makes you feel at peace.
- Walk back to the entrance, look around for your peaceful colour.

The reverse of the card suggested how colour can influence our moods and emotions:

- RED: an emotionally intense colour, it stimulates the heartbeat and breathing. It attracts attention. Red clothing gets noticed.

- BLUE: the colour of the sky and ocean. Blue is the most popular of colours. Blue causes the body to produce calming chemicals. It symbolises loyalty.

- GREEN: symbolises nature. It is the easiest on the eye. A calming and refreshing colour.

- YELLOW: a cheerful sunny colour. It is the most difficult colour for the eye to take in. It helps concentration, it speeds up the metabolism.

- PURPLE: the colour of royalty. Associated with wealth and sophistication. It is a romantic and feminine colour.

- BROWN: this is a solid and reliable colour. It is the colour of the earth. It can be sad and wistful. Often the favourite colour of men.

- BLACK: a colour of authority and power. It can be associated with evil.

- WHITE: symbolises purity and innocence. It is considered a summer colour.

While themed and guided walks work well for some patients, others prefer to walk unaided. I will offer to walk alongside patients who may be feeling agitated or paranoid. Anyone is free to step out of the circuits at any time and to wait with staff while others finish the walk. After walks we gather for refreshments and a time for discussing the experience.

## Further developments of resources

We felt strongly that we wanted to extend the benefits of the outdoor labyrinth and funding has been found to buy two portable labyrinths showing a classical design; the one canvas is 25 feet (7.62 metres) and the other canvas slightly smaller. Within the Trust the canvases are used regularly by patients and staff in a variety of ways. Finding a floor space large enough to host a canvas labyrinth can be a problem but I have found that a gym floor is often the answer.

Here at Ashworth we have a large chapel which has room for the bigger of our two canvas labyrinths. It also has an excellent sound system. With music, tea lights and the peaceful and prayerful atmosphere in the chapel, the setting is perfect. The space is transformed into a 'still point', a place of order in the chaos.

## Expanding awareness of the labyrinth

Mersey Care's Adult Learners' Week 2012 focused on the benefits of mindfulness and mindfulness meditation (3). I was invited to lead some of these meditations on mindfulness and I included a labyrinth walk, which served as a perfect introduction to mindful walking.

For other educational events I have put together a labyrinth workshop introducing the labyrinth with display boards and a PowerPoint of the various styles and examples of labyrinths that can be found around the world. All participants are then invited to walk the labyrinth for themselves. I recently offered this workshop to some of our Trust's activity workers who work with service-users within the community.

## Imposed constraints – maintaining creativity

Any of us who work within a secure setting know that the challenge is to be as creative as possible within the limitations that a high level of security inevitably imposes. Labyrinths are traditionally found in beautiful and aesthetic settings, but within many of our hospitals such a space is hard to find. If boulders, stones or gravel cannot be used to mark the pathways, then box hedges, bark or simply mowing the pathways will work well. If the use of candles is prohibited, as in our case, then LED candles and tea lights are an ideal alternative, helping to create an atmosphere of light and mystery while being safe and user-friendly. I sometimes use a background of calming music which can help to soften and enhance the environment as patients walk.

## Additional resources

The pottery workshop at Ashworth hospital has made two finger labyrinths. These are particularly useful when teaching how to draw a labyrinth. I have a supply of A4-size laminated finger labyrinths which can be used for those who may not be well enough to walk a labyrinth. A check is always needed, for security reasons, before we give out laminated finger labyrinths to certain patients.

## The benefits of the labyrinth for those challenged by mental illness in secure units

The labyrinth is a visual, physical, experiential and beautiful metaphor for the journey towards recovery and mental stability. The labyrinth within our High Secure hospital represents for me a (potential) 'still point' in helping to relieve and turn to positive effect the often turbulent world of troubled minds. Within the forensic setting of medication, analysis, diagnosis and intense scrutiny, in a context where the medical model for the most part reigns supreme, the labyrinth is a symbol of that complementary approach to mental health care and the recovery model (4).

Evidence is indicating the importance of being outdoors. Walking the outdoor labyrinth also fits with 'ecomind', the approach to mental health that upholds the importance of moving freely, and outdoors (5).

In spiritual care, the focus is upon the whole person, upon the humanity of the person, upon their story, upon all that makes them who they are and the often turbulent history that has brought them thus far (6). Where there is a 'mind in a maze' and a sense of self obscured in its tricky coils, the labyrinth experience offers a gentle way to assist the discovery or *uncovery* of that self which is lost. This is particularly important for our patients and service-users on their pilgrimage toward mental health and stability (7).

For our patients within High Secure Psychiatric Services the frontiers between reality and unreality, sanity and insanity, a sense of self and the wilderness of 'no-self', are often blurred and murky. The boundaried pathways of the labyrinth are unambiguous, quite safe, leading directly to the centre. The labyrinth is non-judgemental, there is no right or wrong about it; it requires only the one decision, to walk it or not; it leaves us free to move as we choose and to think what we will; it welcomes us as we are and asks no questions. It offers a place of hospitality for our patients, some of whom have been ostracised by friends and family. The simplicity of its design and the clarity of its pathways provide a welcome contrast to the complexities that many of our service-users face each day. It provides a still point in their turning world and perhaps a moment of healing.

## Acknowledgement

I am indebted to the Revd David Glasson, formerly Head of Spiritual Care, for the ideas for the themed walks and for his support in helping me promote the building of the labyrinth in Ashworth Hospital.

## References

1.  Ashworth Hospital visit:
    http://www.merseycare.nhs.uk/What_we_do/CBUs/High_Secure/High_Secure_Services.aspx
2.  Grace Cathedral: http://www.gracecathedral.org/visit/labyrinth/
3.  For the practice of mindfulness visit:
    www.merseycare.nhs.uk/info/mindfulness
4.  For information on the recovery model of care see: *Recovery and Spiritual and Pastoral Care Services: A Working Model.* Julia Head, 2008. South London and Maudsley NHS Foundation Trust
5.  http://www.mind.org.uk/ecominds
6.  Sewell R. (2008) Holism – remembering what it is to be human. *Complementary Therapies in Clinical Practice*, 14: 75-76
7.  College of Psychiatrists Special Interest Group/Spirituality:http//www.rcpsych.ac.uk/college/specialinterestgroups/spirituality.aspx

## About the author

Reverend Catherine Joy Moon LRAM ARCM BTS worked in the United States for many years. She was ordained at Grace Cathedral, San Francisco, in 1984. During her years of ministry, Catherine has worked in a variety of chaplaincy settings. For seven years she was Port Chaplain to the Ports of the Golden Gate. She then worked among the Hispanic community running a social services centre and place of spiritual support for agricultural workers and their families. Catherine has worked as a chaplain with the elderly, in prisons and in general hospitals and currently is one of the Anglican chaplains on the Spiritual and Pastoral Care Team within Mersey Care NHS Mental Health Trust.

NINE

# The Labyrinth in Stress Management and Self-Care

RUTH SEWELL

> 'By turning our attention inward we gain access to intu-
> ition and wisdom, inner sources of guidance that can
> give us invaluable feedback on questions and concerns
> we carry about our relationships, our work, our health
> and well-being, our spiritual lives.'
> Melissa Gayle West (1:11)

Walking a labyrinth represents a journey, and the nature of my work involves me intimately in the lives of others as they seek to find solutions and new awareness and, ideally, to return to a state of wholeness and healing (2). My professional work is in health care, and since the 1980s I have been a teacher, psychotherapist, and clinical and academic supervisor in the field of integrated cancer and palliative care.

The inclusion of the labyrinth in my workshops started in 2008, after I attended the Veriditas Facilitator training, at Chartres. I realised that while I was an experienced workshop facilitator, promoting stress management, personal awareness and self-caring, for some participants it could remain a behavioural and cerebral experience.

In my personal experience, the labyrinth helps me to bypass the busyness of my mind, lifting me out of patterns of behaviour that keep me trapped in old thinking. For me – and now I know for others – the experience of walking a labyrinth is one that allows for movement into a gentle space, a stillness within, that draws me back to self-compassion, steadies my thoughts, and takes me to a place of heart-centred awareness. I have a growing conviction that while people readily accept and acknowledge the frequent and unyielding domination of stress, they do not remember that the opposite exists – that is, their innate capacity to return to a calm and relaxed state of being, even within the pressure and demands of modern life.

The ultimate aim is to help participants find effective ways to reduce levels of stress, and to explore and develop a daily practice of applying self-help approaches which are capable of helping them to improve their quality of life and well-being.

I host workshops for the public, and specifically for those in the caring professions: health-care practitioners, clergy, counsellors and those in social care environments. Those working in 'health and healing' and ministry backgrounds often disregard their own needs, which leads to burnout or illness. Workshops for colleagues in the caring professions have an additional element, that of recognising and managing their levels of compassion fatigue, which often accompanies deep caring and service.

The labyrinth doesn't impose any expectations or dictate a right or wrong way to follow the path. There are no hard and fast rules, just a respectful invitation to walk at one's own speed and for one's own purpose, with no pressure to perform. It is from this inner space that regeneration and healing can take place.

This chapter will illustrate those things that I consider are important when putting together a day's programme.

## Why focus on stress?

Stress has been described as the extreme end of emotional regulation, an attempt to bring respite and a state of recovery, in order to achieve the natural event of 'the relaxation response' (3). On a daily basis people are heard to cite their own experiences of stress, whether temporary or as a constant source of personal disruption; it has become the 'cultural norm'.

The costs to the whole person can be high; the effect on mind, body, emotion, spirit and social life is immense and insidious (4). Stress is all too easily taken for granted, and therefore not addressed at a meaningful and health-generating level.

## What can such a workshop offer?

In addition to a reflective process, the experiential nature of the workshop invites participants to:
- gradually let go of busy thoughts and motives

- find a quiet place within themselves
- return to an inner knowledge of themselves
- find a place to achieve a state of rest and peacefulness.

The exercises that I incorporate into the workshop are essentially those that relax the body and thus the mind – simple breathing exercises, guided imagery and guided meditations. The participants are not passive to this process. They are invited to share something with the group, something that is important to them, something that holds significant meaning, as a particular window into their lives and 'story'.

When stress is present it creates sensations of restlessness and feelings of constriction, along with tense and tight muscles. Concentration may be poor, and some people feel slightly on edge or anxious and report finding it hard to 'switch off or let go'. The experiential exercises are therefore designed to address and relieve such symptoms.

Over the course of the workshop there is frequently a shift, a switching over, from stress and constriction to those physiological changes that create relaxation and a sense of openness (5). It is vital to introduce the exercises slowly and not too many at a time, and also to use a variety of them. Participants will regularly acknowledge the shift that takes place, which gives the additional benefit of a body and mind awareness that has otherwise been missing.

A labyrinth walk, then, is capable of helping participants to deepen their personal process.

## Experiencing the labyrinth

The reasons and motivations that bring people to such workshops are as varied as the people who attend. Some come out of curiosity, others because they are seeking respite from the demands of daily life, and others hoping to find guidance and answers. Most workshops will include some participants who have never walked a labyrinth, and the first-time experience can be very moving, as it can for those who walk regularly.

> 'The labyrinth walking sessions in our village hall have been of great benefit to me, and, I would say, to all who have come – many with no previous experience.'

For some it is about their spiritual life and its expression. People may not have had opportunity, time or encouragement to start a regular spiritual practice. As Artress reflects, 'hunger for the sacred has reached epic proportions which manifest in different ways'. She offers further that what is often needed is a 'return to a practical spirituality' that is capable of sustaining one's strength, and at the same time encouraging us to find a deepening respect for all beings (6:167/8). Walking a labyrinth for many therefore has led them to find a physical expression of something deeper within, a practical expression of what is 'spiritual' to them.

> 'The labyrinth is a really safe place for me to let go of my thinking and connect with God/Higher power/ universe (whatever language, it's the same thing to me) that is within and without me. At various times the labyrinth has shown me to have compassion for my past, to be more patient with my future and to accept there is a process and a path I simply have to follow; mostly it gives me a little respite from me and a sense of inner peace'. [Senior nurse]

## Treating what happens on the labyrinth as a metaphor

Participants are encouraged to take a non-striving approach when preparing for the walk. Along with the introduction to the walk, there is an invitation to treat whatever happens to them on the labyrinth as a metaphor. A metaphor is a figure of speech that is transferred from its usual context to become a means of understanding another context or experience (7). Most people accept this suggestion and many talk of how the metaphor mirrors their life.

> 'Walking a labyrinth is always different each time but for me there is always a sense of connection with deeper places and truths both within me and in the wider world … At its most marked this feeling can be very profound; at other times it becomes a gentle meditative experience. In a world where many of the traditional metaphors or truths about spirit and meaning appear to have less meaning for many people, walking a labyrinth can be a very important way of connecting with the transcendant and feeding the spirit.' [Palliative care physician]

## Responses to the labyrinth

It isn't uncommon to hear people say that no two walks are ever the same. Some will share that the walk has helped them to calm down or proffered an awareness of themselves that they might not have had before. Some people will walk the labyrinth and find themselves unsettled, which may be unexpected and cause them to walk off the labyrinth, or to appear to be fidgeting or restless as they walk. Some will simply end their walk and leave the labyrinth, whilst others will stay and allow whatever they are feeling to emerge. For those whose expectations appear unmet, or where nothing noticeable happens at the time of the walk, it is helpful to encourage the walker to be patient and to remain open to what might emerge later.

> 'Finding quiet space in modern living is challenging, but finding my own quiet space within a labyrinth was an experience to be treasured'. [Teacher]

For some participants, engaging in the experiential exercises will increase their feeling of tiredness or physical discomfort, which is related to longer-term effects of tension and stress. This happens when they finally stop long enough to recognise just how exhausted or stressed they have become. When discomfort arises it may be easier for them to only partially engage in the exercises, or to opt out of some altogether. Some participants are also very tired, and fall asleep during the deeper exercises. This is not unusual, and all that is needed is to reassure them that they can opt out, or just fall asleep as they need to. When this degree of fatigue is present, it can serve to help the participant to make a stronger commitment to self-care and rest after the workshop.

> '*I believe labyrinths have applications for use in medicine for both doctors and patients as we all need and benefit from the space that this offers.*'
> [Senior palliative care physician]

## Practical considerations

Participant numbers are important, and at a practical level the size of the labyrinth is one of the first considerations. I have two portable labyrinths; one is 18 feet square (5.4 metres) and the other is 24 feet square (7.3 metres). In this type of workshop, up to six people can comfortably walk on the labyrinth at the same time.

My workshops last for six hours excluding breaks, and at any workshop I can welcome up to twenty people.

When I book a venue I am keen to know how much space there is for movement and walking meditations and also the area that is available for the labyrinth to be laid down. It is important to ensure that the group can stay together, so there should be sufficient space for sitting near to the canvas in a non-intrusive, supportive way. I place finger labyrinths in the same sitting areas to be used before and/or after walks. This promotes a sense of supportive community and increases the presence of quiet waiting and stillness. The use of music is often greatly appreciated by participants, but careful thought to the type, tone and level of sound is needed ahead of time. So testing these, and how well the music plays at the venue, should be attempted, if practically possible, to ensure good use of music to accompany the walk.

## Preparation of others and self

No two workshops are ever quite the same. The blend of different people of mixed gender, age and ability, and with or without prior experience of stress management approaches, or walking a labyrinth, keeps the workshops fresh, creative and at times challenging. I prepare myself by keeping practical arrangements as uncomplicated as possible. For example, I do the following:

- Choose a venue that offers privacy and a quiet ambience.
- Make sure that the workshop room offers good ventilation with ample natural lighting.
- Ideally have an additional room/area space for participants who need to leave the main group at any time, if upset or unsettled.
- Advise participants to bring 'layers to wear' to allow for temperature changes, as practising meditations and other 'stilling' exercises reduces movement.
- If there is an opportunity to walk an outdoor public labyrinth, tell the group to prepare for extraneous noise and other walkers.
- In a more secluded outdoor area, let participants know if the walk will take place even if it is raining, or in the event of sun and wind how exposed the site might be for skin care.

*Labyrinth workshop*

## Those participating

### Individuals
Running a workshop requires time and patience. Most adults are capable of introducing themselves and blending in, but I remain mindful of those who might be self-conscious and withdrawn.

### Teams
When leading day events for specific teams or groups of colleagues, other considerations need to be taken into account. Coming together as a team can have the benefit of existing knowledge, friendships, good will, good humour and shared understanding.

Conversely, it is possible that colleagues may feel exposed and untrusting and may not be immediately at ease; some will be concerned about confidentiality post-event.

Respectful boundary-setting can be formalised at the beginning of the workshop, with people agreeing on how they want to relate to each other, including the level of any personal disclosure and confidentiality. In contrast it can also work equally well when it is allowed to be an organic process of letting trust build within an atmosphere of shared (and frequently new) experience, with a levelling of 'permission-giving' over the day.

Preparation is everything. In the course of discussion with the person recruiting for the workshop, it is helpful to ask some practical questions about the usual functions and relationships amongst the team, and the best ways to establish rapport, while still remaining confident of one's own skills in leading groups.

## In conclusion

I have been offering 'Gentle Space' for a number of years and I have discovered so much myself along the way. I have learned to trust myself in the pacing of the guided exercises; knowing that there will be the right mix of people and the right number of people attending at any one time. My experience leads me to remain respectful and confident that I don't have to find or provide answers for participants, but just to make the space and time for them to 'find their own way' – not only in experiencing the guided exercises and the labyrinth walk, but also in finding their own way to respond to that which their heart-mind is asking of them. This process may well start during the workshop, or it may happen later, but I have received feedback that these processes do take place, benefiting the individual and, many times, others as well. The labyrinth is an excellent tool for self-awareness and self-development workshops and I would encourage others to offer such single-day and longer workshops to support and encourage people to find or strengthen their commitment to their life's path.

## References

1. West, M.E. (2000) *Exploring the Labyrinth: A guide for healing and spiritual growth.* New York: Broadway Books.
2. Sewell, R.E. (2008) 'Holism – remembering what it is to be human', in *Complementary Therapies in Clinical Practice*, May, 14:2, pp75-76.
3. *http://www.helpguide.org/mental/stress_signs.htm*
4. Gerhardt, S. (2004) *Why Love Matters.* Hove, Routledge.
5. Aldwin, C. (2000) *Stress, Coping, and Development.* New York: Guildford Press.
6. Artress, L. (2007) *The Sacred Path Companion: A Guide to Walking the Labyrinth to Heal and Transform.* New York: Riverhead Books.
7. Eschner Hogan, E. (2003) *Way of the Winding Path: A map for the labyrinth.* USA, Ashland, Oregon: White Cloud Press.

## Resources

*www.heartmath.org*
*www.compassioninhealthcare.org* which has now become
*www.heartsinhealthcare.com*

## About the author

Ruth Sewell, Ph.D, works as a psychotherapist, Autogenic Training therapist, and lecturer in integrated palliative care and spirituality, offering clinical and academic supervision; her practice is based in south Devon, UK. Ruth is known for her interest in supporting professionals in their own 'self-care' activities and she lectures and runs workshops on the prevention of occupational burnout and compassion fatigue on a national and international basis. Ruth is a long-standing member of the editorial board for the journal *Complementary Therapies in Clinical Practice*. Her work as a psychotherapist focuses on supporting those whose lives are affected by cancer and those living with chronic illness; her doctoral thesis is concerned with the experiences of women during and following breast cancer. *http://www.ruthsewell.co.uk*

The Path Ahead

This is a timely book. In the UK, interest in working with labyrinths is on the increase. We are witnessing a flowering of permanent labyrinth construction and a steady growth in the creation of portable and temporary labyrinths. The number of trained labyrinth facilitators has more than doubled in the last two years alone, enhancing the quality and variety of new projects.

Influencing this development are people with a passion for labyrinths, including those whose chapters make up this volume. Their accounts of personal experience are practical, perceptive and heart-warming and point us to where labyrinth programmes are becoming more established and where future development is most likely.

Work being done with children and young people in our schools, colleges and universities, as well as in families and community organisations, is helping capture the imagination and intuitive faculty at a time in life when the learning process is hugely significant. Skilled, innovative teaching, sound research and sensitive facilitation in these environments should prove foundational, not only for the well-being of today's young people, but for the future of labyrinth scholarship, creation and practice.

The growing recognition that labyrinth-walking is good for our health is also driving notable work in the fields of personal development, counselling and psychotherapy, mental and physical health, and palliative care and bereavement. As favourable research on the benefits for health becomes more readily available, we hope to see further growth in institutional projects and construction, with the labyrinth being increasingly viewed as economically worthwhile and adding clear value in the overall delivery of a more holistic approach to health care.

Woven through many of the chapters is a deep appreciation of the labyrinth as a path for the soul, an inclusive, graceful and safe container for our human journeying. A good deal of interest in working with labyrinths in the UK is currently focused in the area of spirituality. The labyrinth reminds us of the ancient paths and offers a unique and sacred space for exploring new possibilities to nourish our connection with all that gives us meaning, peace and hope.

The editors are grateful for the invaluable dedication, experience and wisdom brought together in this book. We trust that the passion of the contributors will inspire many more people to follow their own paths of exploration in working with labyrinths.

Index

Wild Goose Publications, the publishing house of the Iona Community established in the Celtic Christian tradition of Saint Columba, produces books, e-books, CDs and digital downloads on:

- holistic spirituality
- social justice
- political and peace issues
- healing
- innovative approaches to worship
- song in worship, including the work of the Wild Goose Resource Group
- material for meditation and reflection

For more information:

Wild Goose Publications
Fourth Floor, Savoy House
140 Sauchiehall Street,
Glasgow G2 3DH, UK

Tel. +44 (0)141 332 6292
Fax +44 (0)141 332 1090
e-mail: admin@ionabooks.com

or visit our website at
**www.ionabooks.com**
for details of all our products and online sales